MW00772849

10
Dates
to Your
Soulmate

10
Dates
to Your
Soulmate

A Celebrity
Matchmaker's
Guide from
First Swipe
to Forever

Dr. Christie
Kederian

ZONDERVAN
BOOKS

ZONDERVAN BOOKS

10 Dates to Your Soulmate
Copyright © 2025 by Christine Kederian

Published in Grand Rapids, Michigan, by Zondervan. Zondervan is a registered trademark of The Zondervan Corporation, L.L.C., a wholly owned subsidary of HarperCollins Christian Publishing, Inc.

Requests for information should be addressed to customercare@harpercollins.com.

Zondervan titles may be purchased in bulk for educational, business, fundraising, or sales promotional use. For information, please email SpecialMarkets@Zondervan.com.

Library of Congress Cataloging-in-Publication Data

Names: Kederian, Christie, 1988– author.
Title: 10 dates to your soulmate : a celebrity matchmaker's guide from first swipe to forever / Christie Kederian.
Other titles: Ten dates to your soulmate
Description: Grand Rapids, Michigan : Zondervan Books, [2025] | Includes bibliographical references.
Identifiers: LCCN 2024042393 (print) | LCCN 2024042394 (ebook) | ISBN 9780310369165 (trade paperback) | ISBN 9780310369172 (ebook) | ISBN 9780310369189 (audio)
Subjects: LCSH: Single people—Religious life. | Courtship—Religious aspects—Christianity. | Dating (Social customs)—Religious aspects—Christianity. | BISAC: RELIGION / Christian Living / Love & Marriage | FAMILY & RELATIONSHIPS / Marriage & Long-Term Relationships
Classification: LCC BV4596.S5 K43 2025 (print) | LCC BV4596.S5 (ebook) | DDC 248.8086/52—dc23/eng/20241114
LC record available at https://lccn.loc.gov/2024042393
LC ebook record available at https://lccn.loc.gov/2024042394

Unless otherwise noted, Scripture quotations are taken from The Holy Bible, New International Version®, NIV®. Copyright © 1973, 1978, 1984, 2011 by Biblica, Inc.® Used by permission of Zondervan. All rights reserved worldwide. www.Zondervan.com. The "NIV" and "New International Version" are trademarks registered in the United States Patent and Trademark Office by Biblica, Inc.® · Scripture quotations marked KJV are taken from the King James Version. Public domain. · Scripture quotations marked MEV are taken from the Modern English Version. Copyright © 2014 by Military Bible Association. Used by permission. All rights reserved. · Scripture quotations marked NLT are taken from the Holy Bible, New Living Translation. Copyright © 1996, 2004, 2015 by Tyndale House Foundation. Used by permission of Tyndale House Publishers, Inc., Carol Stream, Illinois 60188. All rights reserved.

Any internet addresses (websites, blogs, etc.) and telephone numbers in this book are offered as a resource. They are not intended in any way to be or imply an endorsement by Zondervan, nor does Zondervan vouch for the content of these sites and numbers for the life of this book.

All rights reserved. No part of this publication may be reproduced, stored in a retrieval system, or transmitted in any form or by any means—electronic, mechanical, photocopy, recording, or any other—except for brief quotations in printed reviews, without the prior permission of the publisher.

The author is represented by Alive Literary Agency, www.aliveliterary.com.

Cover illustrations: Faceout Studio, Molly von Borstel
Interior design: Sara Colley

Printed in the United States of America
24 25 26 27 28 LBC 5 4 3 2 1

To my loving husband, Joah,
and our incredible son, Caleb.

Walking through the journey of life with
the blessing of my boys by my side has
shown me the true miracle of love.

Contents

INTRODUCTION

How to Get Your Last First Date

I sat on the couch curled up with my phone, grinning from ear to ear as I reflected on the phone call I'd just had with Joah. "Not bad for a first phone date," I thought. Then my phone dinged. I smiled when I saw the text was from him: "Hey, would it be weird if I called you again? Like tonight?"

I quickly texted back. "Haha, not weird! I'm free :)"

Joah called me back later that evening, as he said he would, and we talked for an hour. I knew after that second call that I had found someone worth getting to know.

Just so you know this up front, this is *not* how most of my dating went. As a therapist and professional matchmaker for companies like eHarmony, I had learned a lot about dating, and I'd even helped hundreds of people find love. And yet I still struggled to find the right person. Over the last five years, I had tried finding that special someone by going on and off all the different dating apps, to no avail. I felt what many of my clients feel: Couples were falling in love all around me, but for some reason when it came to my love life, Cupid kept missing his target.

I'm a social scientist and researcher, and I knew there had to be a science to it—this process of finding love and connection and alignment with a romantic partner. But I couldn't figure out how to apply that science to my life. So I started my own parallel journey, side-by-side with the matchmaking clients I was trying to help as I went through the dating process myself: first, to learn what I could about the process, and second—*and this is really important*—to prepare myself for when God decided to send me Mr. Right.

What I came to discover about the journey is that it had more to do with *me* than it had to do with the fish in the sea. When I finally understood what was needed for a love that lasts, I put myself in a position not only to find someone but to find the *right* someone and to *be* the right someone so a healthy relationship could thrive.

It Happened One Date

After our second call, Joah and I made plans to meet the next week for our first date. I felt excited and nervous. It felt a bit too good to be true. I had just come out of an "almost relationship" that ended when the guy sent me the all-too-familiar "You're amazing, but I'm not ready for a relationship yet" text after doing nothing but sending me funny memes on Instagram for the last month. I'd known for a while that it wasn't going anywhere, but I still looked forward to the infrequent dopamine hit when he would send me a message. Someone is better than no one, right?

Wrong.

The worst part? This guy I was "almost dating" ended things right before the holidays. I love Christmas, and this guy was ruining my holiday tradition of binge-watching Hallmark movies, which are always best watched with a heaping side of hope. Instead, I was being served twinges of sadness and fear that I'd never find love like those perfect Hallmark characters.

After that, I decided to hit the pause button on dating, since I was deep into finishing my doctoral dissertation. But my best friends from college—"the suities," as we've called ourselves since the days we lived together in the same suite at USC—persuaded me to allow a "positive distraction" to get me through the final lap of finishing my doctorate. The next day, I met my future husband, Joah—on Christmas Eve. (Take that, Hallmark!)

You may read my "how we met" story, and the stories of my clients in this book, and think, "Well, that's nice that it just 'happened' for her." But in reality, it took a long journey to prepare me and my husband for meeting each other and to equip us to embark on our relationship journey together.

As an Armenian-American raised in a Christian household, I had many experiences shape who I am, what type of partner I would look for, and how my dating journey would unfold. Marriage and family have always been at the core of our Armenian ethos. Many aspects of my cultural identity were intertwined with relationships, legacy, and family. Armenian children are often taught about marriage at the same time they are taught about the tragic Armenian genocide, cementing our belief that relationships are core to our survival. Additionally, as a Christian, I believe that relationships are at the center of who we are. We are made for relationship—with God, with others, and with ourselves.

With this worldview, I became fascinated by relationships at an early age. What brings two people together? What helps them decide they want to be together forever? Seeing the examples in my family, especially that of my parents, who are approaching their fortieth wedding anniversary and have the most beautiful, loving marriage I know, helped me have an unwavering belief in love.

I desperately wanted to fall in love, but I ran into the belief, as you may have, that my story had to look the same as the stories of the people around me and that I should look for a certain type of person God would bring into my life in a specific way.

A Formula for Forever

Many people ask me, "So what were the things you did that helped you find love?" As with anything in life, I tell them that the best way to make something happen is to listen to others' stories, learn from their lessons, and apply what you've discovered to your own journey.

Focus on what you can control, and surrender the aspects you can't. Often people focus on lies they believe about dating, which are often things outside of their control, such as:

"Most marriages end in divorce."

"True love doesn't exist."

"All the good ones are taken."

"I guess I'm just meant to be single."

"The right person will come when I stop looking."

"I have to completely love myself and God—and be
happy and healed—before I can love someone else."

I could go on and on.

These messages discourage singles so much that they stop doing what *is* in their power and control to do, including the following:

- Understanding your own past (your origin story) and your own personality to clearly determine who you are compatible with.
- Learning to navigate modern dating by knowing clearly who you're looking for, what your nonnegotiables are, how to ask yourself the right questions for self-reflection after a date, how to make a game plan for a second date, etc.
- Seeking wise and reliable feedback and accountability from those you trust so you don't self-sabotage a promising relationship or engage in negative patterns that prevent you from finding love.

When I focused on myself, doing the inner work and applying the strategies I'd successfully helped hundreds of clients apply to their own lives, love didn't suddenly show up for me. But by taking consistent action, not giving up on love, clarifying my values, and determining who—and what—I was looking for, I was able to find and create the right relationship for me. And I've helped many others do the same.

Now I'm ready to help you.

Done with Party of One

One of the first things I want to tell you on your journey to finding love is this: You're not alone. For much of my journey through singleness, I felt alone. Not just because I hadn't met "the one" yet, but also because I felt there was a social stigma around being single. And if you're single past a certain age, or if all your friends are in a different stage of life than you are, the loneliness of singlehood can be even more devastating because of the resulting loss of friendship and community. It's something many of my clients have experienced, and let me tell you from personal experience—it is no fun! You feel like everyone else—who all seem to be perfectly matched up—is looking at you like you have the scarlet letter (in this case a big ol' *S* instead of an *A*) on your chest.

The insecurity I felt was exactly what many of my matchmaking and therapy clients feel too. For me, the hardest part of being single was going to social events feeling like I had no "news" to share with friends and family. I often felt like my relationship status reflected my worth. As a chronic overachiever, I excelled at everything in life that was mostly in my control. I was the valedictorian of my high school. I earned three degrees from a prestigious university (bachelor's, master's, and doctorate). I had good friends, served in my church, had hobbies I enjoyed, felt fulfilled in my job, and also made time to travel and enjoy life. And yet I sometimes felt the accomplishment that mattered most was having the right someone put their stamp of approval on me. I believed that if I could get an A+ in Soulmate 101, then I would somehow be complete and worthy.

If I was an amazing person and a great potential wife, but no man was here to sweep me off my feet and make me his, was I really worthy?

Every rejection made me feel like my flaws were on display. Maybe I wasn't pretty enough for that person. Maybe I wasn't thin enough. Maybe I was too smart or too educated or too old. The list was endless. In the end, it became easier to see the flaws in the men I was getting to know than it was to accept them in myself or to accept reality: *There's probably nothing wrong, and a whole lot wrong, with both of us. Maybe we just aren't a fit.*

Love Is Never Too Late

Look, dating can be discouraging. Statistically, modern dating is not stacked in favor of those looking for long-lasting love and marriage. You may be picking up this book as a last-ditch effort on a long and heartbreaking journey. But the fact that you are reading these words tells me one important thing about you:

You still believe in love.

I'm proud of you. I'm proud of you for still believing in love. I'm proud of you for still having hope, even if it's just a sliver. You may feel behind on your life's timeline. You may think lasting love is far away. But you're reading this book, so it's closer than you think.

Jesus said that faith as small as a mustard seed can move mountains (Matthew 17:20). The small piece of hope you cling to can move a mountain of discouragement from your past and clear the way for a bright future full of love and joy, unlike the years of struggle you may have come to associate with the dating process.

And hope is a beautiful place to start your journey of finding love.

The key to success in this journey is to approach everything you learn with an open mind. Because of a psychological process known as "confirmation bias," our brains constantly look for evidence that what we *already* believe is true.

This means that if you believe there are no good men left or no good women left, your brain will constantly look for evidence to support that belief.

If you believe you're too old or it's too late to find love and have a family, your brain will look for examples to prove this belief is true.

I'm not asking you to admit you're wrong. I'm only asking you to be open to questioning your old beliefs a tiny bit and see if love can wiggle its way into your life and prove some of your old beliefs wrong.

If you've held on to some of these beliefs for far too long, it's probably for good reason. It's often easier to believe there are no good people left than to make yourself vulnerable and open to rejection once again. But sometimes we let our beliefs keep us stuck, preventing us from trying something new and putting ourselves at risk. Our brains don't like the unfamiliar; they're wired to keep us safe.

On the other hand, if we date differently and with a hopeful mindset, we may just find that the new and unfamiliar is what leads us to the love we've been looking for.

The 10-Dates-to-Your-Soulmate Method

The 10-Dates-to-Your-Soulmate Method, or the "10-Date Method," describes the process this book will guide you through on how to intentionally and consciously go from your first date to understanding if someone could be your soulmate, in ten dates or less. This book will guide you through understanding how to know if someone is the right match for you, while simultaneously deepening your self-awareness. You'll learn how to create the right environment for each date to optimize the process of getting to know each other, which questions to ask, and how to distinguish between genuine red flags and past relational triggers that may need healing.

You may wonder, "Why ten dates?" Truthfully, the number isn't as important as the quality of what happens during the first two months of a dating relationship. In the past, you may have dated someone for two months and not been able to have any clarity on whether they are the right person for you. The 10-Date Method provides a proven, research-backed, and sequential process to take your dating experience to a deeper level and protect against patterns that may have proven unsuccessful in the past, such as rushing into a relationship only to discover red flags after you were already committed, or avoiding relationships altogether and blaming "chemistry" when what was required was to approach the connection in a different way.

How to Use This Book

This book includes a lot of information, and the best way to put it into practice is to read it all the way through and then, when you're in the dating process, come back and read the specific chapter that correlates with the date number you're about to go on or just went on. At the end of each chapter, you'll find sections called "Soul Work," "Strategy," "Tools," and "Coaching Corner," which provide helpful insights based on therapeutic principles as well as practical applications based on my work as a matchmaker and dating coach.

"Soul Work" highlights areas of *yourself* you're going to work on throughout this dating journey. Yes, you want to find someone who will love you for you. But you'll also want to understand how you're wired, what love means to you, and what internal shifts you may need to make. You'll use this understanding to avoid repeating any previous unhealthy patterns and create a new way of approaching your dating life.

"Strategy" lays out actions for you to take along the dating journey. It will help you gain practical guidance and clarity about the purpose of each date, the kinds of questions you can ask yourself and your date, and the types of things you should be noticing. Many people think dating skills develop naturally. The truth is that dating is a skill we need to practice and improve until we find "the one." Strategy will help you change the way you date and give you the confidence and ability to get the result you want: a happy and healthy relationship!

"Tools" is the next step. While "Strategy" gives you the *why* and the *what*, "Tools" gives you the *how*. A lot of dating guidance consists of plenty of insights without the practical instruction manual. "Tools" will help you implement what you learned in "Strategy" in a productive and effective way.

"Coaching Corner" ends each chapter with a quick recap of date ideas, important reminders about what to do and what not to do at this stage, and a strong dose of encouragement.

What's a Soulmate?

Maybe you picked up this book thinking, "I don't even believe in soulmates. How can I find someone I don't believe exists?" When a word or term becomes popular in culture, its true meaning can often be distorted. It's important to differentiate the actual meaning of the word from your opinion of its meaning.

One of those terms is the word *soulmate*. You may have seen this book title and immediately dismissed it, thinking, "I don't even believe in soulmates!"

My belief about soulmates is that, like many things, they are realized only in hindsight. Soulmates aren't found; they are created when you find your person and build a relationship together.

Soulmates aren't quite what romantic comedies make us believe them to be. It's not about finding the perfect person; it's about choosing a person you can grow with, someone with whom you can experience healthy, resilient, enduring love. Your soulmate is the person you'll look fondly at when you're both old and gray—sitting in your rocking chairs and watching your grandchildren play—and say, "Ah, of course it was you. It has always been you."

When we enter the dating process wondering, "Is this person my soulmate?" we're asking ourselves the wrong question. The right question is, "Can I see myself sharing my life with this person on every level—physically, emotionally, spiritually, and financially—and learning and growing with them accordingly?"

So what gets in the way of asking ourselves the right question?

We've been sold a lie.

In my journey to finding love, there were many times when I was ready to throw in the towel and give up. I believed the lie that you could find love by being the damsel in distress waiting in your ivory tower and you didn't have to leave your house.

It didn't help that this was the way my parents met. In our Armenian culture, throughout the centuries, singles have often met their spouse through both official and unofficial matchmakers who set up partners according to their families' values. The inspiration for my career in matchmaking came from the way my parents met—through a family friend who was an unofficial matchmaker. My mom was at home when a knock came at her door. On the other side of that door stood my aunt and another friend-like-family aunt and my dad, the man who would one day become her husband. The aunts had decided that he was a perfect match for my mom, and they literally hand-delivered her husband-to-be right to her doorstep.

If only there were a DoorDash feature for that, right?

My parents have a beautiful marriage and are true soul-mates. But as much as I loved witnessing and hearing about their made-for-the-movies love story, it also set me up from a young age to believe that my husband might just show up on my doorstep one day.

I'm sure there are other stories out there like my parents', but in our era of modern dating they are the exception, not the rule.

Waiting Is a Verb

The other misconception I was sold about finding true love unfortunately came from well-meaning but misguided people in the church community. They sold a version of the prosperity gospel that I'll call the "purity gospel." This was the idea that if you were a good Christian girl, stayed pure, and were "obedient," then God would reward you with a perfect husband and marriage, dropped conveniently on your doorstep so you didn't even have to lift a finger.

My personality and my temperament, combined with my cultural and faith background, created the perfect conditions for me to embrace this purity gospel. In some ways, I'm grateful that I kept my innocence and naivety for most of my early life, as it probably prevented a lot of heartbreak. I'm glad I lived my teen years and young adulthood true to my values. And yet I had a rude awakening when I entered the dating app world in my late twenties. I wish I'd been told to live out these principles for the sake of the principles, not because there was some sort of promise attached to this behavior. The purity gospel caused me a lot of frustration—and, frankly, resentment. I kept wondering what I was doing wrong. I kept waiting, sitting on my hands instead of doing my part while God did his. I struggled unnecessarily in my faith because I kept thinking, "I did all the right things. Mr. Right should be here by now!"

Eventually I—and many women of faith I work with—came to learn that's not the way it works. God isn't a vending machine, doling out a perfect spouse because you've pressed A7 by staying modest and pure. Though that was the message I was sold, I discovered the truth that all along God had a much bigger plan and purpose (and a longer timeline) for me than I ever imagined.

In hindsight, I wanted small, comfortable, and certain. But God wanted a big, grand adventure for me. That was uncomfortable, challenging, and even painful.

If you told me ten years ago that I would write a book about dating, I never would have believed you. "How could I write a book about dating if I've never dated?" my twenty-five-year-old self would retort.

I was the girl who imagined she'd be married with three kids before age thirty. Instead of the "ring by spring," I got the doctorate by thirty because, like many driven women I work with, I decided to pour all my energy—energy that had been stagnating while I waited on God—into my career.

Looking back, I realize that the "waiting" concept contained a damaging message. Waiting for a spouse was often taught as being inactive—sitting at home waiting for Mr. Right to show up—rather than as being active while still trusting. When I was applying for jobs, I trusted, prayed, and waited on God *and* I researched, sent job applications, prepared for interviews, went to those interviews, and sent follow-up emails. It was active waiting. It was expectant waiting. I knew God had a plan. I knew I could trust him, *and* I still did my part. I only wish I had been given permission to do the same in dating.

I'm part of an entire generation of single women who feel like they were sold a lie with the purity gospel and ended up feeling let down by God rather than realizing that they had bought into bad advice. If this resonates with your own experience, I want you to know you're not alone. God wants something better for you.

A Better Way to Date

There's another group of women who have been sold a different lie. In the postfeminist Carrie Bradshaw–esque era, an entire group of women (as Carrie so famously says) have been told that as women, we should be given equal opportunities in the workplace.

And in the dating space.

We should have the opportunity to date like men. To be physically intimate with whomever we choose, whenever we choose. With no strings attached. We should be able to participate in hookup culture, date for fun, and play the field, and in the end we should be able to rise unscathed and ready to walk down the aisle.

This, my friend, is also a lie that single women have bought into. I've seen many heartbroken clients who have lived their lives differently from their purity gospel sisters, but it still led only to disappointment, disconnection, and disillusionment.

Disappointment from experiences that left them feeling jaded about men.

Disconnection from their true desire for lasting love and physical and emotional connection.

Disillusionment with the entire construct of marriage and happily ever after.

Somewhere in here lies the truth: In an era when it's offensive to believe in right and wrong, in a world that emphasizes "living your truth" and "doing what feels best to you," we've forgotten something. While there may not be a *best* way to find "the one," there certainly are *better* ways to look for and build connection.

That's where this book comes in.

With psychological research and anecdotal evidence, as well as a decade of matchmaking experience from working with thousands of singles and going through my own journey, I am here to support you, empower you, and help you become hopeful about finding love.

I want to provide you with a practical and soulful road map that can guide you through the mysterious, confusing, and ultimately beautiful journey to finding love. It's a road map that emphasizes authentic connection—to yourself, to God, and to the person sitting across from you at the coffee shop who's feeling nervous just like you, knees buckling from the pressure, trying not to be overwhelmed by the vulnerable humanness of it all.

They're dreaming of being loved.

Just like you.

Here's to the vulnerable and worthy journey of a lifetime.

One-and-Done or Found the One?

He's a nice guy, but there was no chemistry." I read the text from my client Liz, disappointed but not surprised. In my years as a professional matchmaker, I've seen this type of response to a first date many times. I knew when I matched Liz and Marcus that while they had similar values and both had a desire to build a family, there were some personality differences that, at first glance, would make them seem incompatible.

But I also knew something else that was even more true. I knew that if they were willing to dig a bit deeper, some of those differences were probably things they could work through if they felt the right connection. I'd seen it happen for my clients many times before.

Considering the preferences she shared with me, I knew Marcus wasn't exactly Liz's type. Before coming to me for help, Liz had always dated the life of the party, someone who planned an extravagant and romantic first date, swept her off her feet, and spent hours talking with her, neither of them realizing they'd closed down the restaurant. Liz always fell for the charmer, and who doesn't? But in time, the romantic feeling she'd have after the first few dates would fizzle out, and she'd be left hanging on to an unrealistic dream, hoping the charmer would continue sweeping her off her feet. Sadly, the reality she was often left with was spending the night staring at her phone, hoping for a response to texts she sent that were never answered.

She came to me looking for forever, not another first-date flop.

When I checked in with Marcus after their first date, he said, "I liked her a lot, but she seemed uninterested." After probing further, I discovered that as soon as Liz decided she didn't feel the "spark" or initial attraction that had become so familiar to her, she subconsciously shut down early in the date, removing the chance for Marcus to open up and prove her initial impression wrong. Liz, like many women, assumed her immediate uninterest would go undetected, but Marcus felt the shift. The whole date lasted about one hour, but Marcus knew Liz had already checked out after five minutes.

Finding Your Forever First Date

The pressure we often put on a first date can be overwhelming at best and destructive at worst. We're indoctrinated by romantic comedies and "love at first sight" reality TV that try to convince us that everything we need to know about a person can be discovered on the first date. Our fast-paced society has convinced us that everything from the shirt we bought with Amazon Prime yesterday to chemistry and attraction should show up in an instant. If something (or someone) doesn't grab our attention right away, we move on—and fast. We have no patience to wait for anything, even finding the love of our life.

Poet Mary Oliver, whose writing was often inspired by nature, wrote, "Things take the time they take. Don't worry." In Scripture, a famous verse in Ecclesiastes says, "There is a time for everything" (3:1). And yet when it comes to the dating process, we want to speed things up and figure out on the first date if someone is our forever. We're unwilling to wait out the process and allow the connection to unfold naturally.

We want to know in a second if something will last a lifetime.

Let me introduce you to a girl I know. When we first meet her, she's living a quiet and simple life, doing chores, running errands, her nose frequently buried in a good book. Granted, she's a little bit on the nerdy side, but she's fun and kind, and her community appreciates her uniqueness and individuality, even if she doesn't always fit in.

But her dating life?

It's a little—how do I put this lightly?—disastrous. The one guy in town who has a thing for her is handsome and successful, but she's pretty sure he's more in love with himself than anyone else. The whole situation makes her want to swear off dating forever, but there's still a part of her heart that longs for love.

Unexpectedly, a family emergency takes this girl into

a dark wilderness full of the uncertain and the unknown. In this unfamiliar and scary situation, she meets someone who's as not-her-type as they come. She never would have agreed to a first date with this guy, much less a second. After a first impression gone wrong and some additional bumps along the road, with the encouragement of some friends, she sees another side of Mr. "Not My Type" and realizes there is "something there that wasn't there before." If she hadn't gotten past those first impressions and trusted the journey that this "adventure in the great wide somewhere" was leading her on, she would have missed out on her true love.

If you haven't guessed already, the girl I'm describing is Belle. Yeah, *that* Belle—of *Beauty and the Beast* fame, and one of my favorite Disney fairy tales. While I'm not suggesting you should run headlong into dating anamorphic, tortured, ubercomplicated individuals of a different species (yeah, I know—*all* men are a different species, right?), I do think that on Date One, you have to be willing to go into unknown territory—even without immediate chemistry—and discover what's there.

Soul Work

Understanding Your Emotional Home

Chemistry is either a class you aced (or not!) in high school or an elusive connection that you feel but can't quite articulate. When it comes to the dating process, lack of chemistry is the excuse many people use to avoid going on a second date. A perceived lack of chemistry was the big issue for Liz when it came to her first date with Marcus.

A lot of us are looking for a feeling that can more accurately be described as *attraction* or *connection*. We're looking for a spark. We're hoping to click. What we don't realize is that chemistry—even in dating—ironically has a lot more to do with biology.

When we're initially attracted to someone, our brain releases a combination of chemicals (dopamine, oxytocin, and vasopressin, to name a few) that send us a signal: *Connection is here!* Even though we don't experience what researchers call "adult attachment" until later in life, neural pathways are laid down early on in childhood and are a combination of our biology, temperament, and attachment to our primary caregivers. By the time we reach adulthood and are looking to connect in our other "primary relationship"—finding our life partner—the foundation of neural pathways has already been set.

For those of us who are Chip and Joanna Gaines fans, we've seen the difference between a brand-new home build and an addition. When you're building a house from the ground up, you lay the foundation, and from there, you design the layout and floor plan exactly how you want it. But when you build an addition onto a preexisting house, you often begin with "demo day," where you remove walls or other permanent structures and redesign the house so it flows and feels like that was the original intent and doesn't seem like you simply added pieces like a three-year-old building with Legos.

The neural pathways that developed in your childhood

mind are the foundation for the "house" of your future relationships. Some of us wish we had a mansion on the beach (a stable, loving, and secure upbringing that felt free and spacious) instead of a little bungalow on the side of the freeway (an unstable, chaotic family dynamic that we hope not to repeat with our own marriage and children), but none of us got to choose our childhood experiences. Now you may be trying your best to add on to your house (building your relationship), but it feels awkward and uncomfortable. You feel like you should add a room here or there, but nothing seems to flow naturally. You need a demo day for your brain. This is a process scientists call "neuroplasticity," or the ability of your brain's structure and function to shift and create new neural pathways as it processes and integrates new information and experiences. To attract a healthy partner and change your dating patterns of the past, you have to stop trying to build an addition without first removing some of the permanent structures. Giving your brain newer, healthier experiences will create new neural pathways whereby you can build a healthier and happier "emotional home" for your future relationship than the one you came from.

So, Dr. Christie, what does chemistry have to do with all of this?

Well, I'm so glad you asked!

Chemistry makes your brain say, "Ah, this person feels like home! This person feels familiar! This person fits into my existing place—we can make it work!" But like my mentor and former professor at USC, Dr. Ruth Chung, once taught us, "If they feel like a soulmate at first sight, run the opposite direction!"

The myth we're often sold is that chemistry is the magic wand that confirms you've found your "perfect" match. A turnkey home. No additional work required. It makes us believe that because we "just click," we don't have to do the hard work of building a healthy relationship.

But great marriages aren't discovered; they're built.

Instead, we ought to think of chemistry as one component of a great marriage, but not the only stud the house is built on. Too many homes crumble because they rely on one column to prop up the weight of the entire house. Chemistry is like a load-bearing column. These columns are the ones that, when you're demo-ing the house, you can't knock down because they're essentially holding up the house. Any happy and healthy relationship needs chemistry. Without it, the house will crumble. But chemistry alone isn't enough to keep the whole house up.

Chemistry is what connects. Compatibility (which we'll talk about later) is what makes the relationship last. You need both.

Strategy

Love Is Blind, but Dating Doesn't Have to Be

Most people enter the first date with a list of questions to ask, wanting to get right to the point so they can assess whether this person is someone worth exploring a connection with. What they don't realize is that the approach of entering the first date as an "interviewer" or "investigator" often kills any chemistry that might be there—and reduces any potential for it to develop in the future.

The second wrong approach singles use on a first date is that they go into it blindly. As the saying goes, "Love is blind," but I say dating doesn't have to be.

Before you go on a first date, you should already have some of your main questions answered: Does this person meet the important criteria I'm looking for? Are they also looking for a long-term, serious relationship? Does their ideal future look the same as mine? Yes, knowing these answers before the date would possibly eliminate some people from consideration, but isn't that the point? If you're planning to search for a deep connection at say, a bar, with no information, no pregame data, the odds aren't in your favor.

An essential "strategy" most people don't think about before the first date is knowing what your criteria is before you even start looking for a person. It's important to know what you're looking for in a relationship *and why*. So get out a notebook and a pen (yes, I'm giving you homework in the first chapter—blame the ten years I spent in higher education). Bust out the journal you've been waiting to write in. Open the Notes app on your phone. However you want to capture this, it's time to sit down and reflect on and evaluate your *what* and your *why*.

Here are some questions to help you form the framework that will guide your dating process.

1. What are the top three values or themes that guide your life? These might look something like this: (1) Faith in

God; (2) Connection to family; (3) Career goals. Or they might look like this: (1) Adventure; (2) Freedom; (3) Friendship. Whatever they are, be honest with yourself about what you are prioritizing in your life *today*.

2. What does marriage or a long-term relationship mean to you? (Consider the ways your origin story affects your thoughts about this.)
3. What should this relationship provide you with? What will *you* bring to the relationship? (Be specific here. For instance, what are three things you think you need, and what are three things you think you bring?)
4. What are the three most important character qualities you want in a partner?
5. What are the three most important "on paper," or logistical, qualities you want in a partner (for example, level of education, stable job, height)?

Research says that only 8 percent of long-term relationships start in a bar.[1] Influenced by romantic comedies and pop culture, people want their first date to be spontaneous, exciting, and romantic. It seems like doing research in advance would prevent you from having that magical experience, doesn't it? But we would never show up to a first interview so unprepared, so why would we show up to a first date that way? I recommend having a pre–first date phone conversation or FaceTime chat *before* you invest in going on a first date. If you do decide to go on the date, keep it short and sweet to see if there's a connection.

You don't need to be 100 percent certain about your compatibility after the first date; you just need to be curious enough about who this person is and have enough interest to go on at least one more date to find out.

 **Tools**

Don't Make a Quick Decision from a First Impression

It's a mistake to think that chemistry is an immediate "it's there or it's not" thing that makes or breaks a potential partner's connection. Rather, view it as part of the bigger picture, and assess it accordingly. Put your best foot forward and remain open-minded and curious, even if you're not sure there's a connection. Don't decide until *after* the date whether you want to go on a second date.

I encouraged Liz to look inward before making a snap decision about Marcus. I asked her first to define *chemistry* so that she could see how she was hoping the date went. I also recommended she assess the patterns created in her childhood home that caused her to be an adult who was a bit avoidant and uncomfortable with vulnerability and who attracted emotionally unavailable people as a form of self-sabotage. After further exploring her pattern of making quick decisions based on first impressions rather than giving the other person a chance, we uncovered something about her childhood dynamic with her father. He was always the "fun and exciting" parent, taking the kids out for ice cream and buying them toys they'd been eyeing. But he was also the less consistent parent. Liz never knew if her dad was going to make it home from work in time to show up to her big volleyball game or have an extra hour to help her with homework.

As we explored this dynamic more deeply, Liz told me that because she came from a loving home and didn't seem to have any childhood trauma, she always wondered why she was attracted to men who had no desire for commitment or follow-through and why the chemistry would fizzle out after an amazing first date. I explained to her, like I do to all my clients, that our relationships with our parents can frequently influence the dynamic we're looking for in a dating relationship. Often in our search for a partner, we're subconsciously attracted to the qualities of one of our parents, and it's often the parent we sought to connect with most, even though we may be more similar to our other parent.

Liz didn't have that initial "spark" on her first date with Marcus because he didn't remind her at all of her dad. Often, when we can't put our finger on why someone doesn't feel like a fit, we blame it on the catchall excuse of "no chemistry," when really we mean (whether we're aware of it or not) that they don't have the qualities that could help us resolve our childhood wounds—which all of us have to some degree, regardless of what kind of childhood we had—and give us the happy ending we've always dreamed of.

I encouraged Liz to give Marcus a second chance and look past her initial assessment that they lacked chemistry. Most people don't immediately know if someone is "their person"—much less if they have chemistry—after the first date, and they owe it to themselves to give that person a second shot. That person may not be exactly what they're looking for, but they may be exactly what they need.

Another thing Liz got wrong about her first date with Marcus was her approach and her expectations. She believed the first date told her everything she needed to know about Marcus, and she also falsely assumed that if she didn't have the best first date ever, she shouldn't go on a second date because she didn't want to waste her time. While this assumption is understandable, it also may be what's keeping Liz single. By not wanting to give Marcus a second shot because, in her opinion, it wasn't a phenomenal first date, she may be giving up too early on someone who could be a great match for her.

Why More Is Less

When it comes to dating, the more choices the better, right? After all, how can you possibly know what you like and what you don't like in a person if you don't explore all the options?

Well, according to the research, that's wrong.

In his book *The Paradox of Choice: Why More Is Less*, Barry Schwartz details how, contrary to popular opinion, more choices don't lead to more happiness. Rather, the more choices we have, the longer it takes for us to decide on something—and the less happy we are likely to be with our choice when we finally do decide.[2]

I like to call this the In-N-Out vs. Cheesecake Factory effect. The Cheesecake Factory is a restaurant that has the largest laminated menu I've ever seen, with full photographic spreads featuring dozens and dozens of dinner and dessert choices. There are so many options at The Cheesecake Factory, it should probably be called The Choice-Cake Factory. From Mexican fare to pasta to egg rolls—and, of course, a billion flavors of cheesecake—it often feels like an encyclopedia of food when I flip through their twenty-plus-page menu. But despite having every option I can think of, I've often felt a bit confused about what to order. *Do I feel like tomato basil pasta? Or avocado egg rolls? Or Factory Nachos?* When I do finally end up choosing something (or, more likely, asking the waiter to choose for me), once my meal arrives, I still wonder if I made the best—and *right*—choice.

This is the culinary version of the paradox of choice: I had all the choices available to me, and yet it was difficult to decide—and I wasn't left feeling fully satisfied with my choice. (Thankfully, you can always make up for it with cheesecake for dessert. Because cheesecake, in my professional opinion, does help most things.)

In contrast, think about the experience of going to In-N-Out. When you go to In-N-Out, even though they have only three choices on the menu, you can basically feel your mouth drooling as you anticipate the exact variation of burger, fries, and soda you're about to consume. Without question, you know you're going to enjoy the experience. You don't complain that In-N-Out doesn't have pasta or egg rolls or nachos. You're going for burgers, and you know you're going to like them! And guess what? The length of the In-N-Out drive-through line proves you're not alone! Their menu may be limited, but people still love it. Sure, the burgers are amazing, but you go to In-N-Out because you already know what you want—and you're never disappointed.

The internet and apps are like The Cheesecake Factory, exposing us to more people, more information, and more options than ever before. Want to find a new chiropractor?

Google "chiropractor," and thirty chiropractors within your zip code will pop up. But with so many options available, we're presented with the paradox of choice in virtually every area of life—including dating. Although we have many more ways to meet our potential partner and much more exposure to potential options for who we can date and marry, people are getting married later than at any other time in history—if they get married at all—because having limitless choices doesn't always add up to making the right choice. More roads, in this case, don't lead to Rome. You may have fewer choices with In-N-Out Burger, but you're willing to accept that tradeoff because you know you're not sacrificing clarity or quality. That's the same approach you should have in your dating life: an unwillingness to favor more options over higher-quality options that clearly align with what you want in a relationship.

Don't allow the abundance of options to keep you from valuing the potential partner in front of you. Don't let the lie that "more is better" or "the grass is greener" or "maybe the next person will meet all my criteria *and* be more attractive" keep you lonely, unsatisfied, and focused on things that don't matter.

See the person who's sitting across from you on this date for who they truly are: a precious human created by God to love and be loved. They're not just a number. Not just a list of criteria to check off or an item to order off a menu. Not just a face or a voice. They are a whole person. Maybe they're the one for you. Maybe they're not. But give them the respect and dignity they deserve and don't write them off too quickly because of a first impression that may or may not be accurate. You never know—they may be the one who clicks with you on the next date, and the rest will be history.

Coaching Corner

The date: Make this a midmorning coffee and a light brunch or midafternoon coffee and appetizers. Ideally, this first date is designed to be fairly quick so you don't feel obligated to sit through a meal if it's going poorly.

Ideal amount of time: No more than 90 minutes

Ideal settings: An aesthetic café with a good ambience and fun vibe.

Dos: Listen actively. Be curious. Answer questions honestly without feeling the need to overshare because you want to connect with them. Allow the connection to grow organically.

Don'ts: Don't bring your checklist and ask your date a million questions. Don't talk too much. Don't ask question after question or keep inserting yourself into the conversation, if you notice they're not asking you questions and treating the date like a monologue or therapy session.

Questions to Ask on Date One

- Tell me more about your job and how you got into this field.
- What does a typical weekend look like for you?
- What's a fun memory from your childhood?
- How would you describe yourself as a kid?
- Where is your happy place?
- What is the best trip you've been on and why?

Post-Date One Reflections
- What was something I enjoyed about this person?
- What surprised me about this person?
- What am I curious to learn more about this person?
- What's one thing I would like to know by Date Two to determine if we're compatible?

Don't give up too quickly! Keep an open mind to all the ways love can find you. Just make sure you read the next chapter before deciding if you want to go on that second date!

DATE TWO

It Takes Two (Dates) to Tango

I guess it went okay," Maddie told me after she slouched down on the couch in my office. She had gone on Date Two with Daniel the night before, and while she told me after Date One that she was open-minded, I had my doubts. You see, Maddie wasn't accustomed to going on second dates unless she had an undeniable spark on the first. And with Daniel, the first date in her words was "nothing to write home about," but it also wasn't the worst time she'd ever had. So when I encouraged her to go on Date Two, I wanted her to focus on how she was feeling *and* the fact that he seemed to be exactly what she was looking for. He was kind, intelligent, and funny, but she couldn't put her finger on why she wasn't feeling the instant spark that she used to use as the metric for whether there was enough potential to move forward.

Even though she wasn't sure, I had an inkling as to why.

In my coaching business, Date Two is the place where

I find that many people truly get stuck: they rarely—if ever—go on a second date.

Here's a statistic that sheds a little light on the situation: *nineteen minutes*. That's the average amount of time it takes a single person to decide if they want to go on a second date. That's the same amount of time you spend listening to a podcast at double speed or taking your dog for her after-work stroll. You may be thinking, "Well, that's a decent amount of time to decide if you want a Date Two." But what you may not be considering is that when you say no to a second date, you say no to a potential future relationship with that person.

For Maddie, that was exactly the case. She prided herself on having "good intuition" and being able to "trust her gut." What she didn't realize was that she, similar to my client Liz, wasn't too good at hiding her first impression. So when Daniel experienced her as "evaluating" him when they initially met, it closed him off from being his true fun and friendly self.

"It felt like she was trying to find something wrong with me instead of trying to see a connection. It felt like too much pressure to prove myself," Daniel told me after the date.

If you've seen the popular singing competition reality show *The Voice*, you know what I'm talking about. These individuals are tasked with singing in front of judges who have their chairs turned the opposite direction so they can't see the person when they come onstage, creating a sort of "blind date" scenario. Contestants have one song to perform—and often only the first few seconds of that song—to make a good enough impression for the judges to turn their chairs around, signifying that the singer has advanced in the competition.

Sometimes the singer clearly misses the mark, but other times it's a close call—one where the judges end up regretting not turning their chairs around.

Most of us take the saying "When you know, you know" a little too literally. Whether it's our fast-paced society that encourages us to get what we want overnight with a few quick taps on our phones, or our past trauma that makes us unwilling to hang around long enough to see if we'll get hurt again, the result is clear: We're not waiting long enough for love to show up.

We're not even willing to give it twenty minutes.

Soul Work

Date Two is a critical step, and it's also where I begin to hear statements and questions about the dynamics we bring to dating. We throw around certain words as we turn up the heat on dating opportunities, and we use these words without being granular on how we define them. Let's take a look at what I think of as the three Cs—cognitive dissonance, confirmation bias, and connection cues.

Preventing Cognitive Dissonance Sabotage

There's a danger zone in Date Two territory that I want you to be aware of so you can understand what might be happening in your heart and in your head. Let's say you're giving someone you initially weren't attracted to a second shot.

Sure, sparks didn't fly on the first date, but you're willing to listen to Good Dr. Christie and give Date Two a try. In this step of your journey, you may run into a dangerous troll called cognitive dissonance.

Cognitive dissonance is a psychological phrase for the discomfort we feel when our lives or decisions aren't aligned with our beliefs. We're in conflict with ourselves, acting one way but believing something else. When we repeat a thought over and over, it becomes a belief. And when we have beliefs, we want to stick to them. So we look for, and sometimes create, evidence to prove our belief is true. In the dating process, this can lead to self-sabotage.

In the dating process, cognitive dissonance causes you to believe every thought you have about someone, especially those first impressions that pop into your mind on Date One. When your date walks into the coffee shop, the first thing you think often becomes a belief. You know yourself, right? You don't want to be wrong about someone, so you state your first thought about them and then set out to prove to yourself that you're right. For example, if you had the belief, "I'm not that interested in Jim, but I'll go on a second date anyway just to see what happens," how you *actually* want to complete that sentence is probably, "I'll go on a second date anyway just to see that I'm right about Jim." You're looking for ways to prove your belief right because, well, face it, you don't like to be wrong.

When you go into Date Two with that thought, you will likely self-sabotage. You're looking to prove to yourself that there was no chemistry with Jim, so you'll show up unavailable to cocreate the chemistry needed for the feeling you're hoping for. Like a game of "what came first—the chicken or the egg?" when you go on Date Two after feeling no chemistry on Date One, you have to be honest with yourself and ask, "Did Date Two go poorly because it's not a fit or because I showed up assuming it wasn't going to be a fit and made sure my beliefs came true?"

Confirmation Bias

This process of trying to alleviate our cognitive dissonance, known as *confirmation bias*, shows up frequently when we formulate a first impression of someone. Although most people consider first impressions important and are likely to pay attention to them, research tells us that our first impressions aren't necessarily right and can lead us to make decisions based on inaccurate information and judgments.

In one study on this topic, people were asked to give their first impressions of two candidates for a job and then were given biased information (some positive, some negative) about each candidate.[1] They were then asked to evaluate whether either of these candidates was the right fit for the job. The study found that people only took into consideration the information they were given that confirmed their initial impression rather than taking in all the information and making the best decision based on that.

If we believe we weren't attracted to someone on Date One, we'll look for and pay more attention to the evidence that confirms this on Date Two.

The major internal shift that needs to happen is the realization that you have the choice and opportunity not to believe every thought you think. You also have the choice to go against that belief if you realize it doesn't align with the relationship you long to have and the life you want to live. So give Date Two a chance, being aware that you will subconsciously be looking for evidence to confirm your first impression (whether it was accurate or not).

 ## Strategy

Sparks and Second Dates

As the saying goes, "It takes two to tango," and in my experience as a matchmaker, it also takes two dates to know if you can really "tango" with someone and choose your "dance partner" through life. That's why I encourage all my clients to give Date Two a try.

Why is it so difficult for some people to go on Date Two if a spark didn't start to form on Date One? I believe that those people, like Maddie, are what I like to call One-and-Done Daters. They have no problem meeting people. They have no problem getting asked out on dates. They have no problem asking others on first dates. But when I ask them, "What's the typical number of dates you go on with someone before you decide they're not the right person for you?" the answer I hear most often is, "One."

That's when I know they've earned the title of One-and-Done Dater. There are two types of One-and-Done Daters I want to tell you about.

The First Impression Dater

First Impression Daters are people caught in a loop of thinking that they should just "know" after the first time they meet someone if that person is the right fit, if there's a future, if there's a connection. And sure, you should experience some confirming feelings when you spend time with someone. But often what a First Impression Dater thinks of as strong intuition on their part is actually a limiting combination of premature judgment and subconscious fear directing their love life.

Why is getting stuck at Date Two a common trend? The First Impression Dater typically goes on Date One hoping for *something*, but they don't know exactly *what*. They lack clarity about what they're aiming for. The First Impression Dater lives up to their name, with their vague sense of certainty about their ability to quickly evaluate a dating situation, even when the outcomes keep them stuck at Date One.

The First Impression Dater usually tells me there wasn't chemistry on the first date, or they say, "I wasn't attracted to this person." But when I ask, "Why not?" the answer is typically some version of, "I just know they're not the right one."

If you suspect you might be a First Impression Dater, I want to share a question I asked Maddie and have asked many of my clients that helps provide clarity and perspective:

1. Is there really *no* chemistry, or is there no *immediate* chemistry?

And then I follow up with another question:

2. Is it possible that there is potential for a spark
   to grow?

These questions are important because they force us to
be *reflective*, rather than *reflexive*, about our decisions in dating. It's common to move too fast in our dating lives, moving
from potential to potential without deeper consideration.
We need to slow down and think through the importance of
growth and take time to be able to see things with a clearer
perspective.

When I asked Maddie that question, she paused and
said, "You know what, Dr. Christie, I don't think I've given
anyone a chance when there is no immediate chemistry.
I often figure if it's not there from the start, it won't be
there in the end."

"Are you willing to believe chemistry is something that
can grow?"

She nodded. And I knew she was ready for Date Two.

The Always-a-Bridesmaid Dater

The second type of One-and-Done Dater is the person
who never seems to get *asked out* on Date Two. This can
often be more painful than being a First Impression Dater
because you want to be chosen to go on that second date, but
the invitation never comes. When this happens repeatedly—
when you only seem to go out on first dates with no invitation
of a second date to follow—you're what I call an Always-a-
Bridesmaid Dater. This is pretty self-explanatory: You feel
like you're always the bridesmaid, never the bride, and you're

left wondering why. In the "Tools" section, we'll discuss how to navigate dating when you're an Always-a-Bridesmaid Dater. So don't lose hope; you may be catching the bouquet sooner than you think!

Rate the Relationship Potential

Both types of One-and-Done Daters struggle with another issue I see often. Modern dating has reinforced the idea that "new is better." If you tend to be caught in a cycle of one-and-done dating, you might have a core belief that there's always somebody "better" out there. I like to call this "greener grass" syndrome. This kind of attitude can block you from seeing the great person right in front of you. New isn't always better, and when you're seeking a committed relationship, there will always come a point at which you can choose to focus on one specific individual instead of continuing to scan the crowd. Like I always say, the grass is greener behind the Instagram filter.

Here's another issue that can affect both First Impression Daters and Always-a-Bridesmaid Daters. It's captured perfectly in this quote: "The world is full of sixes who think they're nines and are trying to date tens."[2] If you feel personally victimized by this quote, don't shoot the messenger! I always want to communicate the truth in love, but I also want to serve you, which means I need to serve you some hard truths.

At times, I find myself coaching someone who isn't very ambitious or focused on their career and doesn't make the best financial decisions. We'll call them a six when it comes to money. But they want someone who is successful and driven and is making all kinds of bank. They want a ten—with a bunch of dollar signs behind them.

Or sometimes someone wants a partner who's physically fit and in shape, who lifts and runs and devotes a lot of time and energy to their body. But they themselves would rather be chilling on the couch eating potato chips and watching *Extreme Makeover* instead of committing the time to experience an actual extreme makeover. They want the ten *at* the gym, but they're not willing to give ten minutes *to* the gym.

"If I just find that ten," we think, "I'll be closer to my dream of being a ten." We also might think that being with a ten will validate us. If we can pull a ten, then we've got to be at least a nine, right? "If this ten can love me," we think, "it means I'm worthy enough—or at least look good enough on the outside." It doesn't matter to us that they make us feel like a three on the inside; if they look like a ten on the outside, that's good enough for us.

This strategy is doomed to failure because it bases a relationship on a fantasy rather than on reality—on how you want to live rather than how you truly live. Look, it's great to have goals for self-improvement and to take care of yourself and to throw in a little magic pixie dust too. But when we aren't honest about who we are, and we think a romantic partner can help transform us into our best selves, we put too much pressure on a new relationship that hasn't even had the chance to grow. And when that pressure shows up early, it kills the Date Two vibe fast.

The View from Date Two

So few people get to a second date that I'm often asked, "When I *do* get to Date Two, what do I do?" I usually tell them that Date One is for paying attention to how the person makes you feel, and Date Two is where you begin to explore that feeling and learn more about who they are on a deeper level. Assuming you met online or through a friend, you likely entered Date One with some basic information. The tendency is to go too deep on the first date rather than simply enjoying being in their presence and considering how you feel around them.

Date Two is where you can go a bit deeper and start learning what's behind the first impression. Who is this individual behind their perfectly curated social media profile or attractive dating app photo?

I can already hear a question I know is coming: "But Dr. Christie, do you *always* have to go on a second date? What if the first date made me want to be single for life? What if I already know there's no way I'm going to end up with this person?"

To that I say, I hear you. And while there may be some exceptions to the rule, I almost always recommend a second date. I'll say it louder for the people in the back: Go on the second date!

Unless something feels unsafe or something negative happened on the first date (and we'll be talking more later about red flags to look out for), the only way to get past some of the impatient, idealistic, and, if we're being totally honest, unrealistic ideas we have about dating is to head into Date Two territory with a heart full of curiosity and adventure.

If you're a First Impression Dater, it's time to give the second date a second chance. Subconscious patterns and tendencies may be dictating (and sometimes sabotaging) your opportunity to find love. When you go on a second date as a First Impression Dater, you start to rewire your brain and nervous system to be more *comfortable* with the *discomfort* inherent in the dating process. Look, I get it. It's more comfortable to say no to the second date because it allows you the comfort of thinking you can predict and control the ending, even if the outcome is not what you wanted.

Often we value control more than we value connection.

If you reject your date first, then you don't risk getting rejected. You control the narrative. If you say yes to a second date, you're saying yes to surrender and to uncertainty. You're also saying yes to risk, but risk is the requirement for real love. Remember, your mission is to find the love of your life, and that's going to require a second date. And then a third. And then a fourth. And each of those dates will require more and more risk. Date Two is good practice for your nervous system to become friends with risk.

In Real Time

Let's look at how I helped a few former One-and-Done Daters successfully navigate Date Two while overcoming some issues that had plagued them in the past.

First, let me introduce you to Caroline. Prior to meeting

Brian, Caroline's pattern was stringing together a slew of first dates but never getting asked on a second. The painful thing was, she never knew why. The uncertainty caused her insecurities to run rampant, and she convinced herself she was unlovable.

This tendency is pretty common, according to research dealing with issues of self-esteem. Many women tend to internalize rather than externalize perceived or actual rejection. When someone rejects them, they tend to think something specific about them is being rejected.

Many men, however, deal with rejection by externalizing the reasons, meaning a man is more likely to assume there's something wrong with the person who rejected them. And women, because of our culture's hyperfixation on physical appearance and societal standards that set women up to fail, are more likely to believe that rejection has to do with their physical appearance.[3]

Caroline had bought into this myth. "I guess I'm just not pretty enough," she said as she slumped down on the couch in my office.

"I know it's easy to feel like you're not enough," I told her. "I once saw an interview where Cindy Crawford said that even she doesn't wake up looking like Cindy Crawford!"

Caroline cracked a smile.

I continued, "Let's not jump to conclusions quite yet, Caroline. Let's break down what's happening on these dates."

As Caroline detailed what a first date typically looked like for her, I learned more about what she valued, how she saw herself, and how she communicated that perception of herself to others.

Efficiency and time management were important to Caroline. These values were great when she was in CEO Caroline mode, but they didn't necessarily benefit Dating Caroline. Upon further reflection and processing, we realized she had a pattern that, to her, seemed more efficient than going on a series of dates with the same person. To save time, Caroline would come out of the gates on Date One asking all the hard-hitting questions. In her mind, if all her major topics were covered on Date One (including marriage, theology, future kids, and financial goals), then she wouldn't have to waste time on Date Two if someone wasn't yet ready for all that.

Efficient? Sure. Effective? Not really.

I'm sure you can imagine what those first dates probably felt like for the guys. It was something akin to sitting in a weed-out class at a major university, listening to the professor tell the class that he expects fewer than half of them to still be there by the end of the semester. Not exactly a warm and welcoming environment!

I validated Caroline in her desire to figure things out as quickly as possible. She wasn't wrong for wanting to conserve her time and energy, but I also reminded her that while this strategy might weed out the wrong guys who had the wrong intentions, it was also potentially scaring away the good ones.

It likely sounded to them like Caroline was seeing them as merely a means to an end, a vehicle for getting the husband and family she wanted while achieving her financial goals. It sounded to them like she wasn't interested in them as a person.

What Caroline and many other One-and-Done Daters don't understand is that, at the end of the day, it doesn't matter if your date also wants marriage and kids if you can't stand being in the same room with them for twenty minutes, if you can't enjoy a conversation with them, or if you don't like the person you are when you're with them. They might have all the same goals as you, and they might check all the boxes for faith, marriage, kids, house, pets, and vacations. But if you don't *like* each other, what's the point?

Modern dating has convinced us that if someone is a match for us on paper, we should want to spend our lives with them. The truth is, your list should tell you if a relationship has the potential to go in the right direction, but how you *feel* around a person must match the *facts* of who they are.

Rather than Caroline viewing Date One as an opportunity to get the hard-hitting questions out of the way so she could figure out if she liked the guy, I guided her in reframing her approach, explaining that learning about someone softly and gracefully helps to reveal his true character. Date One is often the place to get the jitters out. Date Two is where we can focus on how we feel about being with the other person and learn more about who they are.

Roller Coasters Are for Disneyland, Not Dating

Next up, meet Alissa. When I started working with Alissa, she was struggling with anxiety about her dating life. At thirty-two, she'd had several dating experiences end poorly, and as a Christian living in the South, she constantly struggled with feeling like she was "past her prime."

She wondered if marriage was in God's plans for her, even though it was what she truly desired. Alissa bought into the false belief that if God wanted her to be married, he would bring the right person to her without any of her own personal effort or action.

In addition to beginning to work with me on her dating life, Alissa was getting support from a therapist for her anxiety. One day she asked me, "Should I wait until I'm truly healed from anxiety to start dating again?"

I responded that healing is a journey and that it happens in the context of our relationships. Our relationship with God helps us heal from our broken relationships on earth. Our relationship with ourselves helps us heal from damaging relationships we've had with others. Alissa's future relationship had the potential to help heal her from past relationships that had hurt her so much.

It's a myth that we can heal in isolation. Many singles believe they are fully healed but the reality is they're not even in the ring. They're sitting on the bench waiting for the elusive finish line of healing to come, not realizing that the medicine is found along the journey.

I don't believe in waiting until you're "truly healed" to date. I know that can be a controversial hot take, but here's why: You won't know if you're healed until your healing is put to the test. I believe in dating *with support*. Having a therapist or coach to help you reflect on your triggers and process them in real time to produce more understanding, and potentially a different way of being, is often where healing happens. You're in the stadium, you're at bat, and you're not alone. You have the support, the insight, and the wisdom from experts and trustworthy counterparts to help you navigate blind spots ahead.

Ram Dass once said, "If you think you're enlightened, go and spend a week with your family."[4] I'll paraphrase this statement for dating: If you think you're fully healed because of all the work you've done on your own, go use a dating app for a week.

I encouraged Alissa to go slowly, but to *go*. We took everything in phases. Downloading the dating app I recommended was a huge step. Learning to swipe through people without matching with everyone. Sending a first message to start a conversation with someone who showed potential. Meeting all these mini milestones helped Alissa feel more comfortable with the dating process than if she had dived into the deep end headfirst. She started to go on dates again, feeling more confident and secure in herself despite her anxiety.

When it came time for us to debrief after her second date with a guy named Clay, Alissa told me she wasn't sure about him. When I asked her why she was hesitant, she told me she couldn't put her finger on it; something just didn't feel right.

"I didn't feel a spark on the first date," she said. "Or the second."

At this point, most of her friends and family wouldn't have asked any further questions, buying into the belief that "when you know, you know," which also means believing that if you don't know, then it's a no. The all-important "spark" is never questioned. How, after all, can we convince someone that there could be a spark—or that there is potential for one to develop—when they didn't feel it?

This ever-elusive spark, impossible to define and different for every person, is single-handedly the most common reason many potentially great relationships end up, as the *Friends* anthem goes, "DOA." Dead on arrival. Cause of death: lack of spark.

But I wasn't going to let Alissa get away with the no-spark argument. I probed further. "Have you ever felt the spark before?" I asked.

"One time," she said. "I felt it when I first met my ex."

Cue the red flag. In my work with Alissa, I'd uncovered that her previous relationship had been incredibly traumatic. Even though there had been an initial spark, with plenty of excitement and an undeniable attraction, the relationship was ultimately emotionally damaging. That spark she felt with her ex? It was the precursor to a dumpster fire of a relationship, the aftermath of which Alissa was still dealing with years later.

Alissa was making a common error I've seen hundreds of people make: She assumed that the initial positive feeling she felt at the beginning of the relationship with her ex should be replicated (you know, the spark), but that this time, with a different guy, the story would have a happy ending. The reality was this: That initial spark she felt with her ex had far more to do with her history and her nervous system. As someone who had struggled with anxiety her whole life, those "butterflies" Alissa felt with her ex were her nervous system ramping up with familiar anxiety. Her brain romantically but catastrophically misinterpreted those butterflies as evidence of being in the presence of soulmate material. It would have been ideal if her brain had interpreted things as,

"Ah, this person feels familiar because they make me anxious. And anxiety is one of my most familiar feelings."

Alissa detailed the emotionally volatile relationship with her ex that often felt like a roller coaster. "Roller coasters are fun for a few minutes," I gently told her, "but no one can live on a roller coaster forever."

She made the mistake many people make when comparing a new potential partner to an old flame. She only remembered the good stuff—including that initial spark—and compared that with someone she didn't have so strong a connection with initially, without remembering that the whole rest of her former relationship was wrong. We can't compartmentalize when it comes to dating. We can't take only our old flame's good qualities and use those as the gold standard, because we've read the whole book, and we know it wasn't as pretty as its cover. Then we make the error of not even trying a book with a not-so-appealing cover because we haven't learned our lesson. We think we can find someone with the same level of spark but without the same level of toxicity.

I dug a little deeper with Alissa. Was it possible that the fact that Clay didn't give her the same butterflies as her ex was a *good* sign?

Alissa remained hesitant. "I was waiting to feel the spark on Date Two, but it still wasn't there," she explained.

"Well, what did you feel?" I asked.

"It felt steady," she said with a whiff of ironic disappointment. "Same as Date One. We had good conversation, we have a lot in common, and we laughed. I also felt like he listened to me."

We checked her list of what she was looking for in a partner and saw that Clay aligned with everything Alissa had said was important to her. And it wasn't just about the list; they seemed to enjoy each other's company. I encouraged her to go on a third date to see what would happen, and she agreed.

What Alissa learned from this Date Two reflection is that the second date provides an important data point. She didn't think Clay was what she was looking for, but he was everything she knew she *needed*: steady, consistent, deep. Date Two wasn't wildly different from Date One, but that was a *good* thing.

When we view Date Two as a data point, we're not necessarily paying attention to speed—how fast that little spark grows or how quickly the relationship is developing. Rather, we're paying attention to direction. Are we feeling more positive, more curious, more peace on Date Two, no matter how small the progress? Are things moving in the right direction?

Alissa didn't feel the butterflies she was hoping to feel on the second date, but she felt something much deeper and more valuable. It felt unfamiliar, which is why it was hard for her to describe.

She felt peace.

Date Two may feel like a time when you're looking for the person to "prove" themselves. Maybe you're looking for them to improve on the first impression you had of them. Maybe you're looking to confirm that they're truly not a fit. What's important to notice after Date Two, though, is how you *feel* around them. Give your heart a chance to settle in and your head a chance to process things from a more reflective and less reactive place. We prime ourselves for butterflies and huge waves of emotion. But peace, quiet joy, feelings of comfort and safety with someone—these are the things that we can misinterpret as a lack of chemistry, or no spark. Actually, though, they could be the exact opposite—long-lasting embers that will fuel the romantic flame for a lifetime.

Started with a Kiss

At this point you may be wondering, "How do I know if we have physical chemistry and when should I find that out?" It's important to first assess your personal boundaries. These may be based on your values, which are informed by your faith or cultural background, or they may simply be personal preferences. It's important to know your *why* behind rules like "I don't kiss on the first date," because that will help you stay committed to your values and boundaries as chemistry evolves.

I don't have a hard-and-fast rule for you on this one, especially if you don't ascribe to a certain faith tradition or principle, but in general, research is clear that the longer you wait to cross into the physical chemistry realm of your relationship, the better. Why? Because it gives you more time to make an emotional investment, which makes it less likely that the neurochemicals and biology will hijack your connection to someone.

Even as early as when we hold hands or give someone a quick peck, the love bubble starts forming around our brain and decision-making processes. Often the physical chemistry and connection accelerates so quickly that it doesn't give the chance for the other more important and more long-lasting types of chemistry to catch up. Take things slowly. The more you delay the physical intimacy, the more you give the relationship a fighting chance to last after the honeymoon feelings melt away.

Looking for Progress, Not Marriage Proposals

Another mistake people make going into Date Two is that they expect it to be astoundingly better than Date One. Their expectations are far too high, and the only direction to go is down. They expect all the sparks that were missing on the first date to light up and all the mysteries that went unanswered to be solved. We're investing a whole second date, after all. Shouldn't we be able to tie it up with a pretty bow and declare happily ever after?

No, we shouldn't.

The only thing you should look for on Date Two is what I call "connection cues." These are essentially little signs that you're moving in the direction of deeper connection. You notice they ask an insightful question that makes you feel truly "seen" by them. They do something thoughtful like remember a detail about your boss you mentioned on Date One. You feel more drawn to and curious about their daily life. The question to ask yourself to assess this after Date Two is, "Was it a little better than Date One?"

In today's era of microwave mentality and one-day delivery expectations, we've become convinced that faster is better. The quicker we know if someone is the right fit for us, the better. We're obsessed with rushing the process.

Just like the impatient, spoiled Veruca Salt from *Charlie and the Chocolate Factory* (the original Gene Wilder version, of course), we want what we want—and we want it *now*. We don't want to have to wait for something to mature and grow.

Date Two is like the first responder for a generation struggling with the virtue of patience, frustrated that they're still in the dating process and don't yet have a pretty Instagram photo to share of a gorgeous destination wedding. It's a way to shift from dehumanizing people with a ten-second scan of their dating profile and a quick swipe, instead telling ourselves, "I see each person as an individual and believe in the potential of love to grow." It's our way of "taking the cue" and believing there could be a deeper connection there, something more sacred than what meets the eye, and committing to explore it further. Date Two is a declaration that potential love deserves a chance to grow. That's why we must look at the facts rather than let our feelings take over the process.

Tools

If You're an Always-a-Bridesmaid Dater

All is not lost for the Always-a-Bridesmaid Dater in the valley of no second date requests. There are some things you can evaluate for yourself because research shows that some behaviors make it more likely for people to get asked out on a second date and that some behaviors could be hurting your chances of having a healthy relationship.

Here's a list of seven things for the Always-a-Bridesmaid Dater to consider:

1. **Your type.** Are you consistently accepting dates from only one type of person—someone who either isn't really looking for a second and third date or may not find *you* to be their type? Subconsciously, you may be going for people who aren't looking for something deeper than a one-and-done date.

2. **Your personal presentation.** You don't need to completely change your look or your fashion sense, but you do need to demonstrate self-care in your personal presentation. Ask a trusted friend or family member, "What's an area of my personal presentation I could improve on?" or "Please rate me on a scale of 1 to 10 in the following areas (such as personal hygiene, appearance, fashion sense, etc.)." I know these are humbling questions to ask, but if you're looking for true, deep, authentic love and you keep getting stuck on Date One, you can continue to experience heartbreak and frustration, or you can give yourself a glow-up. It's up to you.

3. **Your manners.** Research shows that people who have good etiquette (things like chewing with their mouth closed, opening doors for others, and being kind to waitstaff) have a much higher likelihood of getting a second date.[5] Be polite, be kind, be sincere. Bring out your best manners at the coffee shop, because entitled or rude behavior won't get you to Date Two.

4. **Your nonverbals.** Make your date feel like they're the only other person in the room. Most of us have been on

dates where it seems like the other person is looking every-where but at you. In contrast, have you ever felt a special connection where it seems like, even in a crowd, you're the only two people in the room? Even if it doesn't end up working out in the long run, your undivided attention is a beautiful gift to give someone, making them feel important and valued. So pay attention to your nonverbals—eye contact, facial expressions, unspoken responses. They matter!

5. **Your basic interpersonal skills.** Do you show up on time for a date? Do you listen to the other person, or are you doing most of the talking? If you're naturally a talker, aim to say less, ask open-ended questions, and practice your listening skills. You'll appear *more* confident, not less, if you let the conversation flow both ways. Do you have your phone out on the table while you're on a date? Do you speak negatively about other people? Do you bring up previous relationships too soon? These are only a few of the ways we can unintentionally give off signals that we're unaware, distracted, or uninterested in the other person.

6. **Your reality.** Look, I get it. When you're working on your dating app profile, you want to post pictures of yourself that are flattering—and maybe have some filter help. And you want to portray yourself as someone who partakes in cool activities. But the real you and the online you have to be recognized as the same person. Research suggests that most people tend to partake in what's called "strategic self-presentation" when it comes to how they portray them-selves online, including making attributes such as physical appearance, personality, and socioeconomic status seem more favorable than they actually are.[6] This significantly

decreases your chances of getting asked out on Date Two. Why? Because you're demonstrating early on that you can't be trusted.

7. **Your friends.** Ask a friend for some help. And by this, I don't mean the "yes" friend who's only going to tell you what you want to hear. I'm talking about the friend who always tells the truth, in love, even when it's uncomfortable to hear. Explain to them that you're seeing a pattern of not getting asked on second dates, and ask them if they've noticed anything that might be contributing to this. It's not always fun to hear the answer, but what you learn could help you fast-track your way to that elusive next date.

Coaching Corner

The date: Brunch or dinner. If things go well, you can go to dessert after, but don't prolong this date more than three hours.

Ideal amount of time: $1^1/_2$–$2^1/_2$ hours

Ideal settings: A restaurant or café. Avoid noisy or loud settings to prevent distractions and have a chance for deeper conversation than perhaps you had on Date One.

Dos: Be your true self. Be aware of your patterns and tendencies.

Don'ts: Don't show up with your confirmation bias at the ready, whether that's trying to prove to yourself there is a connection with this person or there isn't. There's no need to rush to judgment.

Questions to Ask on Date Two

- What does your ideal workday look like?
- What does your ideal day off look like?
- What's something you've never tried but would love to do?
- Describe your favorite meal.
- What do you like most about yourself?
- How do you prefer to communicate?

Post-Date Two Reflections

- How did I feel around this person on Date Two? How does it compare to Date One?

- What did I find out about this person that was unexpected?
- Are there areas where I can feel confirmation bias creeping in?
- What are some details I don't know yet that would help me understand this person better?

On the second date, notice the little things: Are you feeling relaxed? Are you learning more about the other person? Are you more curious about them? Are you feeling a little more peace about the process?

   If you answered yes, congratulations. You've just had a successful Date Two!

DATE THREE

Third Time's a Charm?

I never feel chemistry with the good guys," Lindsey told me when we started working together. "It feels like everyone I have chemistry with doesn't feel it with me, and everyone who likes me isn't someone I want to be with!"

Before I addressed some of her internal negative self-talk, I wanted to address what the real problem was in the dating pattern she identified. And no, it's probably not what you think.

But first, I have a confession to make: I have a black thumb.

If you picked up this book, looked at my picture on the back, and somehow assumed from that image, "Dr. Christie sure looks like she knows how to garden!" you'd be dead wrong. In my daydreams, though, I'm an avid gardener, cultivating fresh herbs I can cook with and growing beautiful flowers that rival the pretty background aesthetics you see on a random scroll through Pinterest. But no, as much as I love seeing relationships grow, I'm not skilled at helping plants do the same. My maternal grandmother, Annalee, however, was the most prolific gardener. I used to refer to her as the Rose Whisperer because she had the most beautiful rose garden. Somehow they did just what she wanted them to do!

Growing up, I would watch my grandmother tend to her roses with such patience. From observing her, I learned that gardening isn't so much about the flowers themselves. It has more to do with the dirt and the environment. I saw the attention my grandmother put into watering the soil and choosing where she planted the flowers so they would get just the right amount of sunlight. She was a master at creating a perfect environment for her roses to bloom. She once told me, "If a flower isn't growing, we don't blame the flower. We blame the environment."

When we'd walk around her neighborhood and look at other people's gardens, she would point out how this plant was getting too much water or that plant wasn't getting enough. This flower got too much sunlight, and that one too little, and so on.

It was always about the environment. Never about the flower.

By Date Three, when Lindsey felt caught in the same pattern with someone new she was dating named Jake, she mistakenly blamed "chemistry" the same way a novice gardener may be tempted to blame the flower for not blooming.

Observation, Not Expectation

Dating should be more about *observation* than it is about *expectation*. Often we go into the dating experience expecting a lot. We expect someone to meet all our criteria. We expect them to show up as the perfect package, clearly checking off every box on our list without leaving any questions or doubts on Date One and Date Two. And if they don't, we don't even allow the opportunity for the third time to be a charm.

Before Lindsey went on Date Three, I advised her to change things up. "Before you blame the 'flower,'" I told her, "it may be beneficial to observe the environment in which you're hoping the flower will bloom." Change the environment, I told her, and give this blooming flower—this relationship—a chance to grow! It was time for Lindsey to move beyond yet another dinner date into something she hadn't done before.

To know how best to advise Lindsey, I had to dig into the details of what happened on her dates. "It's not that I don't give people a chance!" Lindsey bemoaned. "I go on three, four, sometimes even five dates waiting for something to click, but it never does."

When I asked her what happened on her most recent dates with Jake, Lindsey said, "We go to dinner every time and we talk, but it feels like we run out of things to talk about. It gets boring."

"How long did the dates last?" I asked.

"Well, we've gone on two dinner dates, and each one lasted at least two to three hours."

"So within a span of a few weeks, you're expecting to talk to someone for almost ten hours and not run out of things to talk about?" I asked.

"Well . . . yeah," Lindsey replied. "I guess that seems like a lot of time to spend just talking!"

Lindsey isn't alone in this way of thinking. Many people tend to think that if they spend enough time talking to someone, they'll be able to spot every red flag, create chemistry (hint: the opposite happens—the more we focus solely on talking, the less connection we have because we've allowed less space for nonverbal communication, which is the foundation of chemistry), learn their whole life story, and hear about every one of their future plans.

Sometimes these talking dates end up feeling like an interrogation. We sit the person down at the dinner table until we get all our answers—or else! The problem with this strategy is that the questions we have can't always be answered verbally, and these direct answers often don't give us the insights we're looking for anyway.

To demonstrate this to Lindsey, I asked her, "What are the qualities you're looking for in a potential partner?"

"Beyond all the general stuff, I would love someone who is kind, generous, loyal, and has integrity."

"Great! These are all amazing qualities and so valuable to compatibility in a relationship. So how would you know whether someone is kind?"

"Well, I guess it would be by how they are acting and treating me," Lindsey admitted.

"Right, so not exactly something you could ask verbally."

Next, I asked her how she would know whether someone is generous.

"I guess by noticing how they treat me and how they treat others around them."

The problem with putting so much weight and expectation on those early conversations is that what someone says about themselves isn't always the most accurate representation of who they truly are.

A psychological concept known as "self-preservation theory" asserts that people strategically disclose and conceal the information they share about themselves to create a more positive and socially desirable self-image.[1] This is why we can't always trust what someone says about themselves. It's not that they're necessarily intentionally misrepresenting themselves. But we've all been socialized to try to present the best side of ourselves because that's the only way we believe we'll be accepted and loved.

Think of Date Three as an "on the job" interview for the person you're dating. Make it potentially less formal—and definitely more creative—than an across-the-dinner-table date. It may be the perfect way to learn about their true character in an organic way that they can't necessarily curate. Take a cooking class together, go to a karaoke bar, or try an escape room. The ideas are endless. Research has consistently found that couples who engage in activities together, especially activities that are new and exciting, report increased levels of relational satisfaction.[2]

Don't Give the Playbook Away

At the risk of sounding like a *National Geographic* narrator, I believe we need to observe a potential partner in their "natural habitat." Or in *any* habitat. Far too often, we think of dating as handing off the playbook about ourselves to our date, giving them clues on how to "win" our affection. Right away, we share with them how we like to communicate, how we prefer to interact, what types of dates we like, what specifically we're looking for, and what we disliked about our past relationships.

While it's not wrong for you to be clear about your preferences, the dating process is not about providing your date with a checklist and then seeing how well they fit the bill. What you're looking for is a true connection, someone who values and appreciates the same things in life that you do. You're looking for a person of character. And to figure out if this person fulfills that requirement, you should allow them to feel safe to be authentically themselves. That way, you'll see them for who they truly are rather than who they think you want them to be.

All of us desire to be loved. To find that love, we become accustomed to seeking approval, typically from our parents or caregivers. We also want to be liked. Because this desire to be loved, to be liked, to be approved of, is so strong and innate, we often perform around others. We conform to expectations and play a role we feel comfortable playing, but we may not act the way we truly are.

But performance doesn't give you the clearest picture of what you need to know. How does this person handle hiccups in plans? What's their reaction when a baby two tables away is screaming so loudly at dinner that you can't hear each other over the noise? How do they respond when the barista gets their coffee order wrong? That's the beautiful and surprising thing about love: It's born in the little moments and gestures that make us feel connected and seen. For Lindsey, we'll see how her story with Jake unfolds a little later, but spoiler alert: He was able to charm her the third time around because of the little moments of care and consideration he offered her. Through those little moments, Lindsey could see his genuine heart shining through.

You can't interview for those kinds of insights.

Soul Work

Communication Crash Course

When my client Clara was ready to go on Date Three with Asher, she was focused on uncovering a missing piece she had often overlooked in past relationships. Prior to meeting Asher, she felt that how someone appeared on paper was more important than how she felt when she was with them. She had a pattern of overlooking the little things in past relationships. When a guy she was dating said all the things she wanted to hear, she blindly moved forward, thinking, "He's saying all the right things, right?"

Wrong.

On the other hand, my client Bri had the opposite experience with men. Because of her cultural background, she was accustomed to men not expressing how they felt verbally. "My dad has never told me, 'I love you,' but I would hear it through his actions." While different cultures express love differently, it was personally important for Bri to hear it verbally as well as see it lived out nonverbally. So when she assumed men were interested in her by reading into their nonverbals only, and then the relationships didn't work out, she would be confused.

The truth is, both Clara's and Bri's assumptions about communication were partially true.

You may have heard it said that most communication is nonverbal. But the reality is a little more nuanced than that. The information you communicate can come through the words you say, your body language, your eye contact, and many other modes of expression. For the purpose of this book, we'll refer to communication in the context of relationships and the way you share information about yourself and express who you are, what you're looking for, and what your needs are.

Included in the information you communicate is not just what you say but how you say it. The way you say what you say helps to communicate the feeling behind the sentiment, not just the sentiment itself. Especially for Clara, verbal communication was important, but she needed to focus on how someone said what they said, rather than assuming that their "going through the motions" of saying the right things was enough.

In addition to what we say and how we say it, in our current generation that communicates via screen and texting more than ever, I can't emphasize the importance of nonverbal communication enough. Bri was right about needing to understand someone's nonverbal communication. About 50 percent of communication is through facial expression, body language, vocal tone (the actual pitch you say something in), cadence (how quickly or slowly you speak), sequence (the order in which you say certain words), and much more. Many people assume they are communicating one thing about themselves verbally, when what they are communicating nonverbally, sometimes outside of their own awareness, is a totally different story. Often nonverbal communication is what reveals to us the true nature of a person.

Research has suggested that communication is central to relationship satisfaction over time, so it's no wonder it holds so much importance and value for the dating process as well.[3]

How well someone can communicate their inner world to you is crucial when it comes to evaluating whether they are the right person for you. The fact that the men Bri was dating weren't communicating their feelings verbally didn't mean they weren't having an emotional experience: They simply were uncomfortable with or incapable of putting words to it.

She was faced with a dilemma many of my female clients face in assessing whether a man is the right fit for them. It isn't necessarily socially or culturally acceptable for men to express certain emotions, especially the vulnerable ones. So if someone you go out with on Date Three isn't great at communicating or communicates in a style you aren't used to, it begs the question: Are you able to build a healthy relationship together?

Communication, like many other factors that predict compatibility, is a skill that can be learned. What you're looking for are trends and patterns moving in the right direction. No one is a perfect communicator; often we have learned to express our thoughts and emotions in unhealthy and unproductive ways. What you are looking for is this: someone who is willing to learn and has already begun their journey toward healthy communication.

So how exactly can you self-evaluate whether *you* are a good communicator? In my belief, the mark of a good and healthy communicator is someone who is able to express themselves while also respecting the person they're communicating with.

The five key areas of communication are:

1. How someone speaks to themselves.
2. How someone speaks to another.
3. How someone understands their thoughts, emotions, and experiences.
4. How someone responds to another's thoughts, emotions, and experiences, which is a key part of active listening.
5. How someone adapts their communication style to connect with another.

Some people grew up in environments that were conflict avoidant, where very little, if any, healthy communication occurred, which creates a dynamic in adult relationships where if direct communication is utilized, they feel triggered and overwhelmed. Other people grew up in families where direct communication was the norm, but the communication style was a bit rough around the edges and not as kind as they would have hoped. Or they grew up in an environment where it was difficult to truly be heard. They are accustomed to direct communication and may not realize when they come across as too harsh and need to soften a bit.

Healthy communication in the dating process mainly has to do with being able to express yourself authentically and in a timely, appropriate way that matches the stage of dating you're in.

Many people think they are good communicators if they divulge their full life story, but unfortunately, more information does not always lead to more connection. It's a combination of authentically and consistently sharing information about yourself, over a period of time, that helps to foster a close connection.

People mistake oversharing for good communication skills, thinking it shows transparency and honesty. But oversharing can sometimes be a way to try to create superficial intimacy without allowing the necessary consistent behavior over time to speak for our character. We think that if we share all the details of our lives and engage in hours-long conversations with someone, we are creating an authentic connection with that person. Unfortunately, we often allow the overcommunication to cover the gaps of potential disconnection or incompatibility.

Authentic communication is layered. It takes time, different contexts, and situational information to truly know a person, and even then, we often don't know the whole story.

Strategy

Context Boosts Chemistry

In a fascinating psychological study known as the "bridge study," researchers found that men who were approached by an attractive woman on a shaky bridge were found to experience higher levels of arousal than when approached by an attractive woman on a secure bridge.[4] The men were also more likely to misattribute this arousal to the presence of the attractive woman. The truth is that the men thought they were attracted to the woman on the shaky bridge because of their heightened state of physiological stress. Their anxiety made them think they were feeling attraction when really they were feeling shortness of breath and a faster heartbeat.

We all often misattribute what scientists call the "stimulus" or the "trigger" of our initial attraction to someone. You may believe you're not attracted to someone because of their physical appearance, when it may simply be because you haven't experienced them in a specific context. Context and activity help to boost the neurochemicals in our brain that connect us with someone else. That's *actual* chemistry! If you don't feel those initial sparks, it may be because the environment isn't conducive to generating any sparks. Don't write the person off. Change the environment and see if that helps you feel more connected to them.

The opposite is also true. You may feel like you're truly enjoying your conversation with your date across the dinner table, so you keep talking. But there may be things you need to discover about them that can't be discerned through a dinner-date conversation. That's why it's essential to have a "context date," where you learn about a person in context and see different dimensions of them. The caveat is that you don't want to go on a context date too soon (no hiking first dates, please!) because you do need to have a couple of conversations first to get to know important things about them. Once at least some compatibility is established during Date One and Date Two and you feel a type of connection, then it's time to shift to a context date for Date Three. This is exactly what Lindsey did. When Jake invited her to go indoor rock climbing with him, she was ready and willing to put my theory to the test!

Practicing the "Yes, And"

A context date will put you in a situation where you can learn more about different aspects of a person than you ever could on a dinner date.

Many women I work with ask me, "How do I transition to going on a context date if all my date wants to do is take me out to dinner? What if that's the only thing he suggests? Should I still go?"

My answer is always to employ what I call a "Yes, and" strategy. Yes, you should accept the dinner invitation. In my opinion, as long as you've established that you feel both emotionally and physically safe around them, you should never be the naysayer if someone is gracious and thoughtful enough to ask you out to a coffee or a meal. You should never shoot down their great idea. So that's the "yes." Now, what about the "and" part?

Let's say they want to go to brunch for Date Three. You've spent Dates One and Two sharing coffee or a meal, and you're ready to see how they operate out in the world, not just sitting across from you at a restaurant table. Instead of saying, "No, thank you," to the date invitation or suggesting, "Why don't we go to the farmers market instead?" try this: "I've been wanting to try that brunch place! Thanks so much for suggesting it after you learned that I like French toast. I noticed it's right next to the farmers market. Would you be open to checking that out too? I want to look for a gift there for my cousin's birthday next week and would love to see what the market is like!"

In this way, you're building context into the date he graciously asked you out on. You're saying yes *and* you're being intentional about getting to know him in a different environment. You don't want to waste your time—and his—going on the same date over and over again, learning nothing new. You need a different setting to truly learn who your date is. And if on the first two dates you've struggled to find connection and you're about to chalk it up to a lack of chemistry, Date Three gives you the opportunity to see if it's your date or if maybe it was the environment. Interacting with each other in a different setting gives both of you the best chance to see if there's potential.

Context Leaves Clues

So what "clues" are you looking for on a context date? Well, Nancy Drew, I'm glad you asked!

It's important to pay attention to qualities you see in that person that are more action-oriented. Do they hold the door open for you? Do they walk in front of you or slower than you or do they keep pace with you? Are they kind to everyone they encounter?

These may seem like small things, but they often reveal a lot about a person.

Michela Stevenson, one of the amazing coaches and therapists who works for my company, often shares this example with our clients. Let's say you've been out on a couple of dates with someone who tells you they love kids and want to have children of their own one day. You agree to go on Date Three—a context date—with them where you play mini golf. There's a kid on the mini golf course playing just ahead of you who throws an epic tantrum. This is the perfect opportunity for you to observe your date's response. Do they roll their eyes and become visibly frustrated? Are they compassionate and able to show empathy? Are they able to demonstrate emotional intelligence and not stare or draw further attention to the likely embarrassed and overwhelmed parent? Date Three is where you can see for yourself if their actions truly match up with how they portrayed themselves on Dates One and Two.

When you're on a context date, pay attention to:

- How they interact with the world around them (Do they keep to themselves? Do they greet people they walk by on the street? Do they have a positive outlook on the day?)
- How they interact with people they don't know (Do they interpret someone's behavior in a generous way? Do they see the best in others or assume the worst? Do they offer humor? Do they show empathy?)
- How they interact with people who are marginalized or may be considered "less than" by society (people without homes; people with disabilities; those from an older generation, a different culture, etc.)

- What they notice and point out in their environment (birds chirping, dogs playing at a park, a construction site, a soccer stadium, etc.)
- How they interact with you in different environments (Are they distracted by every person who walks by, or are they able to focus on you despite what else is going on? Do they have spatial awareness and know where you are in relation to them as you're walking through a crowd or across the street? Are they thoughtful about personal space with you and others around them?)

 **Tools**

Situational Conversations

After my client Lindsey shared about the intangible qualities she was looking for in a partner, such as loyalty and generosity, for Date Three I needed to teach her *how* to notice if Jake embodied those qualities without asking direct questions that might not lead to the truth. It would be nice to be able to ask someone, "Are you loyal?" or "Are you kind?" and not get a skewed answer. And a little truth meter, à la *Black Mirror*, held up over their heads, giving us a green light for *true* and a red light for *false*, would also be super helpful, right?

One tool I've developed that I recommend my clients utilize is what I call "situational conversations." In a situational conversation, you ask someone about a specific situation with the intention of learning more about their values and character. Through this type of conversation, you're able to get honest answers without the other person feeling like they're being interviewed. Instead of getting the "right" answer, you'll receive an honest and authentic response—which will benefit both of you.

A good example of this is when you're trying to learn about someone's relationship with money and their personal definition of generosity. You would start a situational conversation by telling them about a situation in your own life, something that doesn't pertain to them. Then notice their response and reaction. You might say something like, "I was visiting my uncle Caleb, and he is truly the most generous guy on earth. One time he loaned me money to purchase my first home, and he was gracious about it. Do you have someone like that in your life?"

If your date's response to Uncle Caleb is one of dismay, like, "Wow, I can't believe he would do that; that's not a good idea," or "Oh, your Uncle Caleb probably isn't very wealthy if he just gives all his money away!" then you have a good idea of what your date *really* thinks about this type of generosity.

On the other hand, he may share a story of a time he did something similar or affirm the value of radical generosity by saying something like, "I have a few people like your uncle Caleb in my life, and they've taught me the importance of being generous and paying it forward."

Engaging in situational conversations during a context date also helps to take the pressure off and avoid getting into an awkward "interview" situation. Let's say you're with your date at the farmers market. You spot a candle you really like and decide to buy it, even though it's a little pricey. What is your date's response? Maybe your date says, "Wow! Thirty dollars for a candle is insane!" Maybe they offer to buy it for you. Maybe they express how much they love supporting local artisans. Whatever their response is, you get some great information without having to go deep sea fishing for it.

Having situational conversations doesn't mean you'll get the exact answer you want to hear every time, nor does it mean someone can't be dishonest with their responses, but it does give you the opportunity to explore someone's values from a different angle rather than having to take their word that they are who they say they are.

Falling in Love at *Word* Sight

One big mistake I see people make in the dating process is they fall in love with, commit to, or become emotionally invested in someone *before* they are able to observe them in context. And then when they see problematic behavior, they're already invested, so they're not as objective as they would have been otherwise.

As the old saying goes, actions speak louder than words. But it seems like in modern dating, everyone's falling in love at *word* sight—with what people *say*. They fall heart-first and don't allow the time and space for their head to catch up. Because we have many ways to communicate via words—talking, texting, DMing, or commenting on someone's social media, etc.—words, in many ways, have become our world.

The popular Netflix documentary *The Tinder Swindler* tells the story of a master manipulator named Simon Leviev, who scammed dozens of beautiful, successful women out of millions of dollars. His primary weapon? *Words.*

It's astounding to see how Leviev's powerful use of constant communication, flattery, and overcommunication prompted women to fall for his scam again and again. Some may say it's a commentary on the challenges of modern dating—that because the bar is set so low, women attach quickly, desperately wanting to believe that a guy who constantly communicates must be one of the good ones.

Through Leviev's texts of flashy photos and expensive travel and his seemingly vulnerable and flattering words to the women he was preying upon, he wreaked havoc in their lives. Because the women connected so strongly with him based on his words alone, they entrusted him with thousands upon thousands of dollars. And here's the kicker: He never spent more than thirty minutes on one date with a woman. *Thirty minutes.* Everything else was done by phone conversations, voice notes, and texts.

Do I believe words are important in developing a relationship? Of course. Are words the only thing that matter in establishing a connection, in verifying the motives of someone's heart, in learning more about who they are? Not at all.

People tend to fall for others too quickly when they assume that because someone is saying all the right things that automatically means they are a good and trustworthy person. In the field of psychology, we refer to this as "overgeneralization." We create factual statements based on all-or-nothing thinking rather than recognizing that there's always nuance in a situation. People aren't static beings, remaining the same over time and in different environments. We have the tendency to want to believe overgeneralizations so that we can feel secure and in control. This is because our nervous system craves certainty and will seek to create it, even if it's not there. This is why we stereotype and "categorize" as a way to assess threat and promote survival. But the reality is that overgeneralizing things often keeps us stuck in our own opinions without being able to see that there may be another version of the truth or another truth that's also possible.

For example, overgeneralization will assume that a person is kind because they asked us questions and were sincere on Date One. Then on Date Two, we go in with the assumption that our date is kind and sincere, so we treat them in the same way, and they more than likely reciprocate. This further confirms our belief that they are a kind person no matter the environment or who they're interacting with— another example of confirmation bias.

If we continue doing this—seeing them as kind only in one context and with one person (us)—we start to form a belief about this person that may or may not be accurate. And so we overgeneralize that they must act this way with every person and in every situation.

When we go on a context date for Date Three, we give our brain the opportunity to continue to learn about this person without falling into the trap of overgeneralizing, either positively or negatively. We have a more logical and cognizant train of thought that goes something like this: "This person was nice on our first dates; I'd love to see if they act the same way on the next date in a different environment."

Climbing the Context Wall

Lindsey finally saw the wisdom in going on a context date with Jake. "Okay, fine, I'll give him one more try," she obliged. On paper, Jake appeared to be everything she was looking for, but she recognized that sitting across from each other at a fancy dinner didn't give her enough information to make an informed decision about whether he could be her person.

After she and Jake went indoor rock climbing, Lindsey and I had a session a few days later to debrief. She was glowing.

"I didn't expect an entirely different side of Jake to come out," she told me. "I'd never rock climbed before, so I was obviously not very good at it, but Jake was gracious the whole time, and it made me connect with him even more. He was way more experienced than I was but so patient. I fully expected him to do his own thing and keep climbing, but he helped me out the entire time, kept pace with me so I wouldn't feel bad, and made it so fun. We laughed together, and I was honestly more attracted to him when I saw him in his element.

"Another thing was that he was *so* funny. I never noticed that side of him in our dinner-date conversations. When he reached the top of one wall, he started singing 'On Top of the World' by Imagine Dragons. I laughed and laughed. And I'd been thinking he didn't have a sense of humor!"

I can't say I was surprised, but I was definitely happy to hear that this context date had shifted their dynamic and helped Lindsey see a side of Jake she never would have experienced had she given up on him after two duplicate dinner dates.

"What else did you notice during the date?" I asked.

"One thing I saw come out was his kindness and consideration for others. He demonstrated a servant's heart. He helped put away the climbing ropes, even though that wasn't required. Oh, and a little kid was blocking Jake's path on one route, but he graciously gave up his spot and hopped down instead of making the kid move. I honestly would've been frustrated if that had happened to me, but he took it in stride. I saw a generous and considerate side of him I hadn't seen before."

I smiled and said, "Well, I guess you had to climb a little bit higher to see the view with Jake is actually pretty special."

Lindsey laughed. She definitely felt on top of the world with Jake on that rock-climbing date, and that context date flourished into a beautiful relationship. They're now happily married, and I can't help but wonder if they hadn't reached the new heights they did on Date Three, if they never would have experienced the love they have today.

Context changed the game for Lindsey and Jake on Date Three, and it very well may for you too!

Context Date Ideas

It's important that context dates occur in a public setting. You don't want to do something like a cooking night at home on Date Three. You need to see how your date interacts with other people and in other environments. Get out of the bubble that includes only the two of you and try one of these ideas instead:

- **Visit an art gallery.** This is a great way to observe how your date acts in a unique environment. It gives each of you the opportunity to comment on something you're both looking at, which can lead to great discussions.
- **Go ice skating.** This is a fun activity where you're able to showcase your silly side and also pay attention to their spatial awareness and consideration of you (especially if your skills aren't on par with Michelle Kwan's). It's also a great place to see if sparks will fly since, especially around the holidays, it can create a romantic ambience.
- **Explore a museum.** This gives you an opportunity to have good conversation as well as interact with your environment while wandering among artifacts, historic archives, natural science exhibits, and the like. (Bonus points if there are interactive exhibits or activities to do together.)
- **Play tennis or pickle ball.** These activities can be great ways to interact with each other while you get to see how they handle competition and their ability to adapt and try something new!
- **Go browsing in an antique shop.** This is a fun way to connect and learn more about someone, since you'll be inspired to talk about their heritage, their upbringing, and their thoughts on history. It also gives you the opportunity to ask fun questions, such as, "What would you do with a piece like this in your home?" or "Did your grandparents ever own furniture like this?"
- **Take a cooking class together.** This is a fun way to learn a new skill, see how you work as a team, observe

how well they take directions, and notice how they respond when they get frustrated (cooking can be hard!).

- **Sign up for a pottery or art class.** This is a fun way to practice your art skills and get a little messy! This helps you to see how seriously your date takes themselves, whether they're able to have fun doing something new, and how comfortable they are with imperfection.

- **Visit a farmers market.** Farmers markets are a great way to interact with someone and learn about their lifestyle, discover what they enjoy or find valuable (handmade items? locally sourced produce? community musicians?), and notice how they interact with the vendors and the crowds.

- **Play mini golf.** This is a great way to see how your date interacts in an environment that may involve the general chaos of kids running around (just how patient are they?). You can also see how competitive they are and whether they can embrace some lighthearted fun.

- **Challenge each other to some arcade games.** Arcade games are a fun way to connect with a potential partner, especially if you're struggling to connect and get the chemistry going. Playing games together can bring out the little kid in both of you. This is helpful especially if they look great on paper but you haven't really seen their fun side yet and are doubting there is chemistry.

- **Take a walk in nature.** Whether it's touring a botanical garden, walking along the beach, or wandering through a local park, what better way to learn about someone than to observe them in nature and see how they respond to the world around them. Do they appreciate their surroundings, or do they seem not to notice the beauty around them? Pay attention to see if they can stop and smell the roses.

Coaching Corner

The date: The focus of this date is *context*, meaning you want to see this person in action. It's helpful to see them in a situation with other people around, so it might make sense for this date to take place during the day, when people are out shopping, running errands, and doing everyday activities.

Ideal amount of time: 3–4 hours (but don't go beyond that time frame)

Ideal settings: See the previous list of ideas. Remember that you want Date Three to be context focused.

Dos: Remember to have fun with whatever activity you're doing. A great context date is one where you forget about how you look and what others think of you and instead are fully present in the moment.

Don'ts: Nightclubs, concerts, or sporting events aren't great Date Three context dates because you'd likely only see how your date responds to the entertainment and you wouldn't be able to interact with your environment.

Questions to Ask on Date Three

- Who is your favorite person?
- What's a pet peeve of yours?
- If you were a city (based on your personality), which city would you be?
- What was your first job?
- What did you enjoy the most and the least about school?

Post-Date Three Reflections

- How did I feel around this person while seeing them in a different context?
- How does that align with what I felt on Dates One and Two?
- What did I find most attractive about this person on Date Three?
- Using what I noticed on Date Three, what am I curious to get more information about?

Let's see the chemistry that context brings in Date Three and discover just how charming the third time can be!

DATE FOUR

Four Better or Worse

I'm not sure we're compatible."

If I had a nickel for every time someone used compatibility as the reason for the demise of a potential relationship, I'd have a *lot* of nickels.

Audrey came into my office after Date Three without the warm glow I had witnessed after Dates One and Two with Chase.

"What came up on the date that made you feel incompatible?"

"Well, we went on a context date, hiking around a nearby lake, which was a lot of fun, but he talked a lot about how much his family enjoys camping and road-tripping in their RVs, and I can't see myself using up my hard-earned vacation days to rough it in the wilderness. I'm more of a glamping, five-star hotel, evil stepmom Meredith in *The Parent Trap* [Lindsay Lohan version] type."

I laughed and said, "Well, I hope your own future kids don't leave you on an air mattress in the middle of the lake like they did in *The Parent Trap*!"

She gave me a half laugh, but I knew deep down she was worried that the chemistry and attraction she initially felt with Chase were fading fast. Audrey was facing what many people subconsciously question around Date Four—the million-dollar question: Are we compatible?

As a dating coach who's worked with thousands of singles, I can attest that after the excuse of there being "no chemistry," compatibility is the next most popular scapegoat for a relationship ending before it truly had the chance to get started. But what does compatibility even mean? Most people don't know, but it *sounds* like a good reason, so they use it as a deciding factor.

By Date Four, you've likely established that there is chemistry with someone, and now you want to observe whether there is true compatibility. Contrary to popular opinion, compatibility and chemistry are two very different things. Chemistry has more to do with the connection you feel with someone: According to research, chemicals are involved in attraction. Your pheromones emit certain chemicals that activate the brains of some people, but not necessarily others.

In the research on chemistry by world-renowned anthropologist and author Dr. Helen Fisher, she found that people have genetic predispositions that draw them to each other.[1] In another study, a Swiss zoologist asked a group of women to rate the smell of T-shirts worn by various men. The women tended to rate as more pleasant the odor of men who happened to have a different immune system setup than their own. Scientists concluded that women were subconsciously choosing a different genetic makeup to provide the favorable outcome of "genetic resistance for their offspring."[2]

Compatibility, on the other hand, is all about the similarities you share with someone. It's about how well two pieces of a puzzle fit together. According to research, although there are various dimensions of compatibility, the more similar you are to your potential partner in important areas—like values, background, and goals—the more compatible you tend to be.

My definition of *compatibility* is "the measure of alignment you have with another person." It seems simple, but it's quite layered when we take a deeper look. You're not going to be *completely* compatible with anyone. Even the most connected couples have some areas of incompatibility. But you should be compatible in the most important areas with the person you're considering being in a long-term relationship with.

Once you feel a connection with someone, are curious to get to know them better, and have the desire to continue that process, it's now time—on Date Four—to assess more deeply the measure of alignment this person has with your personality, your temperament, your values, and your lifestyle.

Dr. Neil Clark Warren, the founder of eHarmony, is one of the leading experts on compatibility[3]—a tenet on which he built the foundation of his dating app. Many dating apps have followed his lead in implementing a similar algorithm to connect people with others who match them in a variety of areas. In their research, eHarmony identified various "dimensions" of compatibility.[4] These dimensions fell into three general categories, which are important for you to be aware of as you navigate the process of figuring out if you're compatible with someone.

Dimensions of Compatibility

Physical Attraction

The first component is physical attraction. It's what we usually feel when we first see someone and feel a "spark." Audrey and Chase both felt that instantly for each other.

"I thought his photo was cute on his profile, but seeing him in person instantly queued the butterflies for me! I could tell he was attracted to me as well by noticing the way his eyes softened when he looked at me in conversation."

Psychological Compatibility

The second dimension of compatibility is what we call "psychological compatibility," which essentially means that your temperaments, your core values and beliefs, and your communication styles are aligned. For Audrey, she felt Chase was her "psychological twin flame," as she called it. She felt like he "got" her. Their upbringings were similar, they were both the ones bringing the joy and connection in their families, and they were both the reliable ones in their friend groups. They shared a sense of optimism, a desire for adventure, and an ambition to build something of great impact in the world. She'd never felt so "in sync" with someone. Check. Check. Audrey and Chase were two for two when it came to these dimensions of compatibility.

Interpersonal Chemistry

The third category is interpersonal chemistry, which is where Audrey's question of "Do we have enough in common?" was rooted. This area of compatibility is about shared hobbies, interests, and experiences that draw us closer to each other. Interpersonal chemistry is also at the root of many friendships. As C. S. Lewis writes of friendship, "Friendship is born at that moment when one person says to another, 'What! You too? I thought I was the only one.'"[5]

While Audrey believed that because she and Chase didn't share enough interests in common, and they didn't share Chase's particular joy of camping, it wasn't quite the dealbreaker she thought it was.

On Date Four, it's important to ask questions that help you understand how compatible you truly are:

1. How do you see the world?
2. What is your balance of passion and self-control?
3. Do you ascribe to traditional gender roles? If not, what do you see a potential partnership looking like?
4. What degree of closeness and intimacy do you desire in a relationship? Do you value autonomy more than connection?
5. How empathetic are you?
6. How do you see the world?
7. How do you process experiences?
8. How do you approach relationships with people?
9. How do you handle compromise and set boundaries in your relationships?
10. How pragmatic are you?

11. How do you deal with frustration?
12. What does your typical day look like? How does this reflect your lifestyle and values?
13. How do you curate your home environment?
14. Are you active or do you tend to identify as a "homebody"?
15. How would you describe your communication style?
16. How did you behave as a child, and how does that influence you now?

The Compatibility Cure

Audrey was worried that because she and Chase didn't match in every area of compatibility, they did not have what they needed for a healthy relationship. The truth is, compatibility must be taken into consideration on multiple dimensions because you may be aligned in some ways with someone but not in others. The most important priority is to match with someone on your core values, your temperament, your personality, and your goals for the future.

In addition to various levels of compatibility, couples can have chemistry without compatibility, and they can have compatibility without chemistry. This begs the question, Which one is more important? But that isn't necessarily the right question. The right question is, Can you be patient and willing to see if both chemistry and compatibility will grow? In contrast to what romantic comedies want us to believe, both chemistry and compatibility take time to build with someone.

Survey Says

When I worked at eHarmony, I helped clients fill out surveys to determine their compatibility with another person. The questions were typically assessed on a scale of 1 to 10 to determine how much they agreed with certain statements. I always recommended that clients choose an answer on the extreme end of the scale only if those things were *very* important to them. For example, if a client's top value was spending their relaxation time at home, I would advise them to prioritize it highly on the rating scale.

Now, my client might also like going out from time to time to have fun with friends as a way to unwind, which is great, but it wasn't as important to them as where their true enjoyment and recharging occurred: at home on the couch.

The reason I walked my clients through the survey in this way is because we tend to weight criteria as equally important when in fact there can be important differences for us. For example, maybe hiking is a huge part of your life. You're into hiking, most of your friends are into hiking, and it's something you make time for every weekend. You spend so much time hiking that it would probably be a point of conflict and disconnection if your partner never wanted to go hiking with you. So your hiking hobby carries a lot more weight for you than it might for someone who says they like hiking just to sound interesting on their dating profile, but they haven't gone hiking in a year. You don't want to downplay what's truly important to you, and you don't want to rate everything as very important when it's not.

Let's say that in addition to your commitment to hiking, you like to be clean and organized generally, but you're not rigid on that value. You're fine with a little clutter here and there, and you don't mind a little mess—because who has time to clean when you're so busy hiking! But let's say you've put cleanliness and organization right up there with hiking on your survey answers. If you put too much weight on someone's organizational habits while truthfully those habits don't bother you too much, that can stand in the way of true compatibility with someone because you're focusing on a quality that doesn't matter that much to you.

Have you ever had a relationship end because of one of the dimensions of compatibility mentioned previously? If so, this is likely an area that will continue to prove incompatible in other relationships as well. For example, if you believe strongly in traditional gender roles, and in the past you've dated multiple people who did not ascribe to those same beliefs and this was often a reason that a relationship didn't work out, it's likely that traditional gender roles is a personal area of compatibility you need someone to share. You don't want to date another person who doesn't share those values and hope that maybe this time will be different.

Soul Work

No Guarantees in Love, Only Green Flags

"Is it going to last?" Allison asked me. She was feeling great about Stephen but couldn't handle the anxiety of not knowing if it would last. She wanted to keep her heart open to love, but could she move forward without the certainty?

I wanted to soothe her anxiety, to tell her of course it would last. But I knew I couldn't give her that assurance. No one could.

In the modern dating world, it's tempting to be so focused on certainty and wanting to know if a relationship is going to last that we have a hard time enjoying the love we have right now.

We want a love we can see going the distance.

We want a love that's predictable.

We want to know that love will last forever.

Why? We don't want to be hurt. We want to protect ourselves. We don't want to be blindsided.

Someone can show us every green flag in the book, but there are no guarantees in love. What we *can* look to are predictable patterns and complementary dynamics that increase the likelihood of long-lasting love.

And that's what I told Allison: "Don't look for guarantees; look for green flags."

Instead of wondering if a relationship will last, focus on recognizing two important green flags. The presence of these green flags signals that the relationship has the elements needed for a genuine connection.

Here is the first green flag: You'll want to see if the person you're getting to know is compatible with *anyone*, not necessarily just you. Do they have the character qualities and personality to build a healthy relationship in general? Often people only look for ways someone is compatible by asking, "Do they check all my boxes? Do they have a stable job? Do we have the same hobbies?" We can be so focused on the ways they're compatible with us specifically that we don't see the ways they're not ready for a healthy relationship in general.

If you see a green flag in this first area—their ability to have healthy relationships in general—*then and only then* can you move on to the second area.

The second green flag to look for is whether they're compatible specifically with you.

This differentiation is more important than people think. If we don't first consider if someone is a good match for a healthy relationship in general, then we're going to look for ways they connect with us or seem like they "get" us or "complete" us. Instead, we need to be asking ourselves if they can form a healthy relationship with *anyone*. Someone ready for a healthy relationship demonstrates healthy relationship-building traits, like good communication, kindness, empathy, commitment to connection and growth, and loyalty.

But if we focus *only* on the fact that they seem like they can be in a healthy relationship and don't specifically assess whether they are compatible with *us* in particular, we'll feel like we're unmatched in the relationship. An unmatched relationship, even between two healthy partners, may produce an unhealthy and unhappy dynamic if there are core differences.

For example, for someone to have compatibility with you, core components of their upbringing will likely be similar to your upbringing. Someone who doesn't have the same financial background as you (let's say you grew up in a wealthy family and they didn't) might not be incompatible with a relationship in general but could run into some challenges in a relationship *with you*. Differences often create misunderstandings because we are trying to translate parts of ourselves to someone who may still be learning our language, since it's not their native tongue. This is why research on compatibility asserts that while opposites may attract, people who are similar in important ways often enjoy the healthiest, happiest, and longest-lasting relationships.[6]

It's important to note that no two people are perfectly compatible in every way. But you want to be as compatible as possible in the important ways and trust that if those core components are there, you can work through any areas of incompatibility. Focusing on important elements of personal compatibility with someone creates the opportunity to build trust and safety, where differences can be celebrated instead of merely tolerated.

Deposits in Dating Compatibility

What every couple should focus on—and doing this early on in the dating process will give you a head start—is the ability to build goodwill. This is essentially building emotional "savings" into your relationship's metaphorical "account." When you're compatible with someone, you're able to cultivate goodwill from the start of your relationship, and from there it will only grow. When difficult times come and when disagreements happen (and they will), you'll have built enough emotional savings to withdraw from when times are tough.

The way you generate deposits for this compatible savings account is by aligning in important areas of compatibility as much as possible before the relationship even begins. Then, when the differences come up, they won't overpower the connection and the mutual trust that have been built.

Let's paint a picture of what I'll call (for all you Charles Dickens English lit fans) A Tale of Two Couples:

Let's just say "it was the best of times" for couple A when it came to financial compatibility. They both grew up in families that viewed and used money in similar ways. Their families were frugal and believed in saving their money and living economically. Having this similarity is like putting deposits in the bank for couple A, pun intended.

In the future, when couple A has a disagreement about a financial decision, as they are bound to have at some point, they will be operating from the same mindset and belief system about money that they inherited from their parents, whether they ascribe to it or not. They're operating from the same manual, so it's much easier to navigate inevitable disagreements and withdraw money from their account because there's actual money there.

Couple B, on the other hand, come from backgrounds with different beliefs about money and the proper ratio of spending versus saving. This starts them out at a metaphorical deficit when it comes to compatibility, because there isn't the mutual sense of understanding that comes from having similar backgrounds and experiences.

In the future, when couple B has a disagreement about a financial decision, they will be operating from different worldviews and upbringings. One partner grew up in a household that lived to work; the other grew up in a household that worked to live. Operating from a different worldview causes disconnection and other challenges that prompt the couple to attempt to withdraw from a "bank account" that is empty because they don't have the deposits of compatibility to withdraw from. They are stuck in a disconnect of values and are unable to get back to a place of harmony because of this core incompatibility.

I'm *not* saying that having areas of incompatibility means you're not supposed to be together. Instead, I'm saying that the more areas of compatibility you *do* have, the more goodwill you will build to buffer the inevitable areas of incompatibility that arise in any relationship. What you don't want is to have so much incompatibility that you don't have a chance to build goodwill because you're constantly in a state of disconnection over your differences.

Date Four is where you begin to measure the compatibility and goodwill you already have that can lay a solid foundation for the relationship that is forming.

Strategy

Date as the Person You Are, Not the Person You Want to Be

Because compatibility is so critical to a successful relationship, you need to arrive at Date Four as your true self, with the values, disciplines, challenges, and areas of growth you have right now, not as the person you think you want to be. Many people think that if they date someone with the qualities they aspire to have, then through osmosis they'll acquire those qualities. Regarding goals and career aspirations, you've likely heard the saying, "Dress for the job you want, not the job you have." But when it comes to dating, you should date as the person you are, not the person you aspire to be. On Date Four, show up clothed in who you really are. Be intentional about showing up authentically as yourself, not a version you think they'd like—and pay special attention to compatibility.

When Selena first came to work with me, she was struggling with showing up as herself instead of as who she wanted to be. Some of her top criteria were that the person she wanted to date should be financially stable, physically fit, and very healthy. However, when I asked about her own lifestyle, she revealed that she was struggling with finances and loathed exercising. She hoped that if she attracted someone who embodied who she *wanted* to be, she would somehow be inspired to change the things she didn't like about herself.

The reality, I told her, is the opposite. One of two dynamics typically emerges when a person dates someone they aspire to be rather than someone with similar values and habits:

1. Admiration becomes resentment. Admiration for the ways the other person is different from you in positive ways slowly turns into resentment that you're not as healthy, financially stable, educated, successful, or active as they are, and that resentment seeps into your relationship.

2. The desire to change what you don't like about yourself turns into feelings of shame in their presence. You think this person will motivate you, but at times, that motivation feels like shame. Their strength in that area seems to amplify your own weakness.

Even though I was a matchmaker, researching compatibility and helping match clients based on their compatibility at eHarmony, it was still difficult to assess which areas of compatibility truly mattered to me in my own dating life. Over time I realized I was weighting certain components, like chemistry, quite heavily. But eHarmony's list includes many other dimensions of compatibility, all of which are important parts of the dating puzzle. I realized I was over-emphasizing the importance of one of the dimensions of compatibility, and part of me didn't believe it was possible to find everything I was looking for in one person. The tough question I had to ask myself is now the question I encourage every person I work with to ask: "When I overemphasize the importance of this one area of compatibility, am I neglecting the other pieces of the puzzle?" For example, am I falling into the false belief that if we didn't have chemistry instantly, then the other components of compatibility don't even matter?

Core Values

Different dimensions of compatibility develop and are discovered at various points in the dating process. In other words, some things just take time. For example, if we look at the three areas of compatibility discussed previously—physical, psychological, and interpersonal—we may notice that these develop and grow during different phases of the dating process.

Physical attraction is typically discovered fairly early in the process, but deep psychological compatibility takes more time. In my dating life, I had physical attraction to and interpersonal chemistry with several men early on, learning about their hobbies, interests, and shared experiences, but their core personality traits were revealed only after I'd gotten to know them better and had enough time to evaluate whether their character remained consistent over time.

Each individual has to decide for themselves which dimensions of compatibility are more important. We have to make peace with someone else's priorities as well, even if we don't agree on some things or we operate with different worldviews. Having mutual respect for differences, along with knowing when they are too much for our relationship to handle, is key to the process of discerning if someone is a match for you. The secret to building a healthy relationship is knowing which differences you can work through and which are so at odds with your values and the life you desire to build with someone that they can't be overlooked or worked through.

This is what occurred when I was getting to know Kyle. Introduced through mutual friends, we shared a lot of compatibility on paper: same values, same background, same faith. We were driving back from our third date when he told me he didn't think I "energized" him in the right way.

Somewhat surprised to hear this, I wasn't sure what he meant. In hindsight, what I came to realize is that Kyle, whether he knew it or not, was referring to an area of compatibility he likely valued and felt was important to be aligned in—what eHarmony refers to as "emotional energy." It's a component of emotional temperament that describes "how spontaneous, vivacious, outgoing and adventurous you feel on a regular basis. How often you need to recharge and are your happiest when you are doing something."[7]

Kyle lived a low-key life and felt it was important to recharge his emotional energy. While I valued alone time as well, I had a full social calendar, with tons of friends and activities. And I enjoyed filling my life and calendar in this way, with not much white space. I had never paid attention to this dimension of compatibility in my dating life up until that point. But for Kyle, this was important. Having time to recharge likely was a core value for him.

This doesn't mean that recharging in different ways means you're incompatible with someone per se. What it does mean is that there are going to be some areas of compatibility you believe are more important than others, and the more in alignment you can be with a potential partner in those areas, the less conflict you will likely experience.

Though I didn't imagine it would be very important to me, I found out that what eHarmony calls "traditionalism" was very important to me. I was raised in a Christian and Armenian household, and my love for tradition and for upholding both my cultural and faith-based values ended up being a very important shared trait that I looked for in men

I considered dating. For me, it went beyond whether they shared my faith or cultural background. I cared more that they viewed their own faith and cultural background with reverence. When I met men who were more progressive, contrarian, or antiestablishment, I felt a lack of alignment and connection. It's not that I was attached to the institutions necessarily, but I did want to respect tradition while carving my own way. Those who were ready to throw out the baby with the bathwater or who had critical views of tradition were going to be in for some rough sailing if I chose them to be my partner.

It took a while to realize it was important to me to connect with someone who valued going to church, taking part in cultural events, and raising children to know and understand their heritage and faith background. In hindsight, navigating modern dating with traditional values was quite the challenge. Still, I'm glad I was discerning in my process of choosing someone who shared these values with me, not just someone who "checked the box" of faith and cultural background. I now realize how much goodwill this choice has created in my marriage, because tradition is core to my lifestyle and now is part of the life my husband and I are creating together.

Like Tevye, the father in the beloved musical *Fiddler on the Roof*, says in the song "Tradition," "Because of our traditions, everyone knows who he is and what God expects him to do."[8] That's what tradition meant to me. I knew it was one of my core values because through that tradition, I felt secure in my identity and faith.

The Four Cs of Connection

When considering connection in potential romantic relationships, many people may not have clarity about what the four
Cs of connection are, how to identify them, and how they
play out in the dating process.

Chemistry

The first C, as we've discussed in previous chapters, is
chemistry. We can even feel what we consider "chemistry"
with people in a nonromantic setting. For example, when you
meet a new friend, the feeling you get is a version of chemistry or "me too" that helps connect you with them.

Compatibility

In contrast, the second C—*compatibility*—is the alignment between two people based on identity, personal values,
and goals for the future. In a scientific sense, compatibility
is the opportunity for two things to coexist without conflict
or problems. As shown in my work with Selena, she had to
be honest with herself about her financial state and her own
health and fitness because otherwise she'd enter a relationship where conflict would arise due to her spending habits
and lack of understanding about money. She needed to find
compatibility with a partner who could share similar values
and lifestyle habits. If Selena tried to be in a relationship with
someone who was financially savvy and very fit and healthy,
that person would struggle to coexist with her because their
values and lifestyle habits would be too different. Discovering

if you are compatible with someone is similar to seeing if you can coexist and thrive in the environment and dynamic the two of you create.

Complementary

Many people confuse compatibility with the third C—*complementary*. It's a huge mistake many people make when they're assessing if someone is a good fit for them. *Complementary* is the feeling that someone is the yin to your yang, that they fill in the missing piece that you don't have. While this dynamic can work well in some aspects of your relationship, it flies against the wisdom of research on compatibility, which states that while opposites may attract, couples who are similar are the ones who tend to last. If someone embodies all your weaknesses, this will create a relationship that is frustrating and causes resentment at best or one that lacks understanding, empathy, and alignment at worst.

But it's helpful to be complementary in some areas. For example, my husband is the handiest Mr. Fix It I've ever met. He can fix something in a minute that I've been trying to twist and turn for an hour. On the other hand, I am tech savvy, while he doesn't even use social media. Another area we complement each other is in the realm of hospitality and hosting parties. We make a great team, and we enjoy our respective roles. We both love being around others, but I love providing the entertainment and making sure everyone is happy and enjoying themselves. He loves flexing his creativity in planning the menu and ensuring everything is organized and running according to schedule. We each recognize how our gifts and skillsets contribute to the overall vision and goal we've set together.

Being complementary, not in the theological sense but in the psychological sense, is like the example of the church given in the Bible in 1 Corinthians 12. The body is made up of different parts, and everyone has their specific role, so no one should feel inferior. Everyone's role is essential to keep the body functioning as it should.

Joelle and Mike were compatible and complementary at the same time. They had similar values and visions for their lives. Aspects of their personalities complemented each other. They had some differences, but that mostly made their relationship interesting without being chaotic. Mike was what Talia Goldstein, founder of the matchmaking company Three Day Rule, calls the "rock" in their relationship. As a CPA, he was steady, solid, and dependable. He wasn't the life of the party, but he had a quiet confidence that put everyone at ease. As the life of the party, Joelle was the "star" in the relationship. She felt comfortable with the spotlight, and Mike loved shining that light on her. The way they complemented each other created a lot of joy and fun in their relationship while allowing each person to truly embody their full self and not have to dim their light, like they would have had to if both wanted to be the "star."

Chasm

The fourth C is what I call the *chasm*. This tends to be the most problematic area we come across in the dating process. When two people vary too much in chemistry, compatibility, or complementing each other's characteristics, this creates a significant gap that will almost always compromise the relationship. This is where we see dating relationships fizzle or romantic relationships fall apart. The couple didn't build enough of the first three Cs of chemistry, compatibility, and complementing each other, and now the chasm feels too wide to bridge.

Compatibility Check

When you're assessing compatibility on Date Four, keep in mind the three specific areas of compatibility—deep psychological compatibility, interpersonal chemistry, and physical attraction. For Joelle and Mike, they had established physical attraction on Date One and interpersonal chemistry on Dates Two and Three. On Date Four they began exploring their psychological compatibility and learned that their temperaments, their core values and beliefs, and their communication styles were aligned, giving them a big green light to move forward.

Physical Attraction

Physical attraction may seem like it should be immediate, but you may notice different feelings emerging during Date Four than on Date One. You may feel more attracted to the person as you get to know them, or you may have initially felt an instant attraction but find it fading as you spend more time with them.

Psychological Compatibility

When it comes to assessing deep psychological compatibility on Date Four, I recommend paying close attention to your date's temperament, especially if you're doing an activity together:

- Do they seem high-strung and particular, or do they go with the flow?
- How do they handle things going wrong or inconveniences popping up?
- How would you describe their outlook on the date? What is their general tone in conversation (optimistic, cautious, skeptical, brave, fearful)?

You may still be seeing only glimpses of their personality and character, but as with a puzzle, each section you put together will help you eventually see the whole picture. Also as with a puzzle, it's important to have the box in front of you while you're putting the pieces together. If you can't see the full picture, you may feel stuck or think you finished the puzzle just because you finished one section.

Too often people put one section of the relationship puzzle together and think they've completed the whole thing. They don't have the entire picture in mind. They think because these two pieces are together or one section of the puzzle is in place, they don't need to finish the rest. Or they believe it will be completed when they're officially in a relationship.

But we need to put together more pieces of the puzzle than we think before we're in a committed relationship. We can't just put the edges together or put all the blue pieces in a corner and say, "I'll worry about those later." Too often I see engaged couples whose relationship is an unfinished puzzle that they thought would sort itself out. Research has found that 69 percent of the arguments couples have are over what are called "unsolvable problems"—conflicts in marriage that never get resolved.[9] Once you're married it's important to learn to accept the things you can't change, but my guess would be that most people are stuck in unsolvable problems within their marriage because they didn't finish as much of the puzzle as they should have *before* they tied the knot.

I don't want that to happen to you, friend, which is why assessing compatibility date by date, as you keep the puzzle box in front of you, is the best way to determine if someone could be a match for you. I'm not saying everything will be perfect, and sometimes puzzle pieces that look like they should fit end up not being a good fit at all.

As I advised Audrey on Date Four, the incompatibility she was worried about wasn't necessarily unimportant, but it wasn't enough to rule out the entire relationship *yet*. By showing up on Date Four authentically as herself, not pretending to like camping, and by learning more about other areas of interpersonal chemistry where they *were* compatible, she would be able to paint a clearer picture of whether their incompatibility was a chasm or simply a difference to be celebrated.

If you can stay consistent and persistent in learning about a person, you may be genuinely surprised at how delightful a feeling of connectedness can be. It will be worth the wait, it will be worth the work, and it will be worth the risk.

Interpersonal Chemistry

When it comes to interpersonal chemistry, hobbies, interests, and shared experiences are all important considerations. Date Four is the perfect time to explore more deeply how someone's hobbies and interests shape their personality and lifestyle. "What would my daily life look like with this person?" is a great question to keep in mind on Date Four. For example, on Date One you may have learned that they enjoy attending concerts. On Date Four, you realize attending concerts isn't just something they're interested in, it's a core part of their life. You learn they have season tickets to the Hollywood Bowl and integrate live music into time they spend with their friends, who also frequently attend concerts and value live music as an important component of their lives.

In my experience, a lack of shared hobbies only tends to become problematic in relationships in which someone treats their hobby like they're in a committed relationship with it, which makes their partner feel like they're a third wheel. I recommend having at least one shared hobby but not over-prioritizing shared hobbies to the point that other aspects of compatibility become less important. Having different hobbies can create excitement in your relationship, foster a sense of curiosity, and give you the opportunity to learn from each other—and about each other—in unique ways.

Tools

Deep Dive Questions

I recommend three types of questions on Date Four:

- **Observation questions:** Now that you've gotten to know this person a bit, asking an observation question can be a helpful way to go one layer deeper and find out more about who they truly are. For example, "You're such an upbeat person. What do you think helps you stay so positive?"

- **Vulnerable questions:** Asking your date to dig one layer deeper can help you understand their level of self-awareness. For example, "What's an embarrassing story you don't tell many people?"
- **Mindset questions:** Date Four is an ideal time to learn how this person views the world and to discover their mindset and their overall perspective on life. For example, "Are you a glass-half-empty person or a glass-half-full person and why?"

Coaching Corner

The date: Date Four is a combination of conversation and context, a blend of Dates One, Two, and Three. If you want to go to a movie or a comedy show, great! Just make sure there's time for focused conversation before or after, and make sure you pay attention to context clues, such as experiences that reveal personality traits, throughout the date.

Ideal amount of time: 3–5 hours

Ideal settings: Consider doing something that involves one of your hobbies or interests.

Dos: Notice early signs of compatibility and ask, "Are there green flags that encourage me to move forward?" Of the three areas of compatibility (physical, psychological, interpersonal), which seem to be aligned? Which are you unsure of?

Don'ts: Don't plan a date where there isn't time for conversation. Also, Date Four shouldn't be with friends, even if you are doing an activity.

Questions to Ask on Date Four

- You're such an upbeat person. What do you think helps you stay so positive?
- What's an embarrassing story you don't tell many people?
- Are you a glass-half-empty person or a glass-half-full person and why?

- Who's someone you look up to and why?
- What movie or TV character do you most relate to and why?

Post-Date Four Reflections
- Does this person seem to be consistent across the dates we've now shared?
- Are they bringing the same kind of curiosity and interest to our dates that I am?
- What expectations have I been bringing to these dates that may have more to do with the person I think I want to be than with the person I am today?
- How am I feeling: Anxious? Unsure? Peaceful? Interested? Excited?

The more authentically you show up on Date Four, the more you can accurately assess whether a promising future relationship with this person is on the horizon. Moving forward from Date Four requires trust that the work you're doing to assess compatibility and build a solid foundation for your relationship will keep you going through all that lies ahead.

DATE FIVE

Familiar Isn't Forever

L ike many singles I work with, Kelly came to me knowing a little bit about what psychologists refer to as "attachment style" or the way we connected to our parents as children and how that mirrors how we connect as adults in romantic relationships. Being single for several years, Kelly told me she "definitely had a secure attachment style." The online quiz told her, so it must be true, right?

I shared with her a little-known fact that although you may think you're securely attached, you possibly haven't truly put that attachment style to the test because when you're single, you're avoiding the triggers that come when the possibility of disconnection is present. How do you date when you're afraid of getting hurt? Or how do you share your true feelings when you're not sure someone feels the same? *This* is where you learn your true attachment style, which then can help you understand where you're getting stuck.

In my experience working with singles, Date Five is the place where attachment style–based triggers come alive because that's when our fears and vulnerabilities tend to sabotage a budding relationship. On Date Five, it's time to notice if you feel the desire to speed up the emotional intimacy and connection, or if you feel the need for independence and distance because the potential for deeper connection is making you feel too vulnerable and you're afraid of getting hurt.

While *attachment style* has become a popular phrase in modern dating, most people don't truly understand where it shows up in the dating process and what effect it has, so here's a quick summary of the styles and my take on how they affect your dating relationships.

There are typically four styles of attachment: securely attached, anxiously attached, avoidantly attached, and disorganized attachment. Though it's important to be aware of all four, for the purposes of Date Five, I'm going to focus on the anxiously and avoidantly attached types because these two seem to rear their heads and sabotage a potential connection.

People who are *securely attached* hit the jackpot because their temperament was a match for their parents' style of parenting and their needs were met. Their parents were likely responsive to their needs and taught healthy communication and gave them a safe place from which to learn how to be independent. They feel comfortable with the balance of intimacy and independence. They trust others and themselves and have positive self-esteem and feelings of self-worth.

Those who are *anxiously attached* have a stronger desire for intimacy and closeness rather than independence because their parents either were hyperconnected and overbearing or were inconsistent. They often believe that separation or independence is abandonment or a threat. They seek constant validation from partners and can become overly dependent, and sometimes codependent, in relationships.

Those who are *avoidantly attached* have a stronger desire for independence than intimacy. Their parents were likely more dismissive and misattuned to their emotional needs, causing them to disconnect and learn not to rely on someone else. They often have difficulty connecting with and expressing their own emotions, and they prioritize autonomy.

And those who have *disorganized attachment* essentially combine both anxious and avoidant tendencies and alternate between desiring intimacy and then pulling away into independence. They likely experienced childhood trauma such as abuse or neglect.[1]

Attachment wounding refers to the way that our attachment styles trigger us in relationships. Typically, in relationships, the more we desire *connection* over *independence*, the more anxious we tend to be. The more we desire *autonomy* over *intimacy*, the more avoidant we tend to be.

Before Date Five with Gabriel, Kelly fell closer to "anxious" on the spectrum between anxious (wanting to connect more than detach) and avoidant (wanting to pull away more than lean in) because of the way she bonded with her parents.

On Date Five, you may notice that you now desire closeness and connection with your date. You pay more attention to whether your date is leaning in as much as they have in the past or if they seem less engaged. Typically, I recommend a longer date around Date Five that combines both context and conversation, which is the type of date Kelly had with Gabriel: a nice dinner and a gallery opening. Kelly was able to explore what extended time and conversation with Gabriel felt like to her nervous system. She believed she was "securely attached" until she noticed a sense of anxiety come over her because she deeply longed for connection and commitment, even though she wasn't entirely sure if Gabriel was a match for her yet. She found herself mulling over every interaction: Was he looking at the attractive girl across the art gallery or at the painting? Did he seem quieter than on their last date? Was he not asking her enough questions? She quickly realized that her anxious attachment was rearing its head because her desire for connection and leaning in overrode the desire for independence and "playing it cool."

 **Soul Work**

Preventing Attachment Self-Sabotage

We don't fully understand the implications of our attachment type until we truly care about someone else. Up until Date Five, Kelly was still trying to determine if she liked Gabriel and if he was someone she wanted to form an attachment with. Date Five is usually when attachment issues show up, because that's when we start to develop deeper feelings for someone. We can't have attachment triggers if we're not yet attached to someone. When Kelly realized she wanted a deeper connection with Gabriel, she suddenly looked a lot like someone we're about to meet: Anxious Annie.

Meet Anxious Annie

Contrary to what you might assume, there is no "wrong" attachment style. Knowing your attachment style is merely a tool to better understand how you relate to others. You can't go back to your childhood and change how younger you, with your unique temperament, interacted with your environment. Instead, what you can do is be aware of your origin story and show up with loving acceptance of the younger version of yourself. You can discover any innocent but incorrect ways you may have tried to get your needs met as a kid. Then you can use that knowledge to prevent yourself from repeating patterns you built in childhood.

If you're what I call an "Anxious Annie," your attachment style tends to be more insecure and veer toward anxiety. You likely desire connection over independence. You may sit by the phone, refreshing your screen and ensuring you have a good signal to make sure you didn't miss a text from the guy you like. You may obsessively research them on the internet, so much so that when they mention their aunt while you're on a date, you almost say out loud, "Which one, Marsha or Kathy?" Anxious Annie wants connection, and she wants it now! But there's a danger zone to be aware of here. When you want connection this bad, you might create it artificially or falsely believe it's there.

A mistake anxious people make is believing that attachment style develops and changes in isolation. It doesn't. Attachment style happens in the context of relationships. The good news is that even though the triggers happen in a relationship, the healing does as well. People often try to work their way into secure attachment on their own, whether by reading books or journaling or doing other forms of self-development work. While this can be helpful, the real test comes when you put that work into practice and try to connect with another person. *Whom* you choose to attach to is the number one thing that can shift your attachment style.

The more avoidant someone you're dating is, the more anxious you might be. If you're not anxious at all when someone ghosts you, that means you likely didn't care in the first place. But before you diagnose yourself with an anxious attachment style, make sure you're not dating someone who isn't remotely interested in you!

Our nervous system can usually identify when someone isn't interested or available. It sends a signal that says, "I recognize this!" It recalls times we've felt rejected or abandoned in the past. It's up to us to decode that signal and discover whether familiarity is going to work in our favor or not.

While all of us can usually identify as feeling anxious when someone we like appears not to be interested, Anxious Annie values connection so much that she often unintentionally simulates emotional intimacy and looks for an opportunity to connect and commit too quickly. She'll overlook any potential red flags because more than anything she wants to feel connected and loved, even if it's by the wrong person. She's also eager to commit to someone early on, because the uncertainty that's a normal part of the dating process feels too dysregulating for her. Once she develops feelings, she has a deep desire to define them. She does all this because she longs to feel safe, but she could be compromising her actual long-term emotional safety. True safety in a relationship comes from getting to know someone deeply and consistently over a period of time, ensuring their actions match their words. In her hurry to escape the uncomfortable feelings of uncertainty, Anxious Annie risks giving her heart to someone she can't possibly know all that well yet.

Just because someone feels familiar doesn't mean they should be your "forever." Sometimes a dynamic from your past isn't one you want repeated in your future.

As we walk through the process of finding our soulmate, we often must do the work of breaking generational patterns and trauma that have been passed down to us from our parents and grandparents. As Kelly learned on Date Five with Gabriel, her anxious attachment required her to form a new normal for her nervous system to truly thrive and heal in relationships. It isn't fun to work through deep generational patterns while navigating murky dating waters, but this is exactly the time when these conversations emerge from the deep, and you want to have clarity on the dynamics you bring to a dating relationship.

Meet Avoidant Ava

Avoidant Ava sees *everything* as a red flag. Her thumb is sore from swiping left on every guy (but she always has her reasons). By Date Five (if she can even make it that far without running the other direction), she can usually see potential with someone, but fear tends to rear its ugly head and find something to be critical about. Date Five tends to be where Avoidant Ava expands her objection game, trying her hardest to self-sabotage what could be a good thing.

"I noticed he has a weird smile."

"I don't like the way he eats sandwiches."

"The fact that all his texts are green bubbles because he has an Android is bothering me more than it should."

"I'm attracted to guys with facial hair, and I know he would grow it if I asked, but I want a guy who would do it on his own."

To which I always ask, "Did that bother you before?" Nine times out of ten, Avoidant Ava didn't even notice his smile bothered her on Dates One through Four—because it probably didn't. If something pops up on Date Five that was already present but didn't bother her before, we almost always know what the culprit is: her avoidant attachment style.

The moment Avoidant Ava starts to feel like she wants to connect and be vulnerable with someone, or when she realizes she could be developing deeper feelings, that's when everything changes. Her subconscious—and her nervous system—says, "Don't let your guard down, and don't show any signs of weakness because you're only going to get hurt." Avoidant Ava doesn't trust people easily because she's been let down before. Early on in life, she learned to depend only on herself and not the people she was supposed to trust, because they weren't available or able to meet her needs. Now, years later, it's ingrained in her system that when she feels at risk, the safest thing to do is shut it all down.

Whenever I encounter an Avoidant Ava in my coaching practice, she always has what she sees as a good reason to reject someone. She'll say something about his hair or his teeth or declare that there wasn't chemistry. She thinks she's articulating what the problem is, and it's always something about the other person, but it's simply evidence that she doesn't know how to identify and define the true reason for her hesitancy. Her group chat full of close girlfriends will text her seemingly supportive words like, "You go, girl—never settle!" But deep down, the truth lies in the pattern. She will *always* find a reason to stop a possible relationship at this stage because if she starts having feelings for someone, she runs the other way out of fear of the potential to get hurt again. The guy may seem nice, safe, and genuine, but to Avoidant Ava, going past Date Five feels like going past the point of no return.

Avoidant Ava knows that opening up more on Date Five risks pain and heartbreak. But as C. S. Lewis says so perfectly, if we don't risk getting hurt, we risk much more:

> To love at all is to be vulnerable. Love anything and your heart will be wrung and possibly broken. If you want to make sure of keeping it intact you must give it to no one, not even an animal. Wrap it carefully round with hobbies and little luxuries; avoid all entanglements. Lock it up safe in the casket or coffin of your selfishness. But in that casket, safe, dark, motionless, airless, it will change. It will not be broken; it will become unbreakable, impenetrable, irredeemable. To love is to be vulnerable.[2]

Avoidant Ava may believe it's easier not to give her heart and her love to anyone, but what she doesn't realize is that remaining resistant to true connection and vulnerability is fundamentally changing her. In an effort to avoid heartbreak, she's losing her softness. Sometimes she wraps herself in "little luxuries," as Lewis writes, and those little luxuries are often the efforts and extremes she goes to in an attempt to protect herself. She may prioritize strict and superficial criteria that don't have much to do with compatibility and long-lasting happiness.

You may be an Avoidant Ava if:

- You've made excuses like "I'm too busy to date."
- You quickly find faults and errors in potential matches and are unwilling to tolerate imperfections.
- You write off certain ways of meeting people ("I won't use dating apps" or "I won't go to a singles' event").
- You tend to be a First Impression Dater and feel like you just "know" when someone's not right for you.

The key thing to pay attention to during Date Five is whether you have any feelings that seem to come out of left field, including emotions that you didn't have previously. Rather than a response to an actual problem, these new feelings may be more an issue of allowing your attachment style to sabotage a good thing.

If you've seen the Pixar movie *Inside Out 2*, you're likely familiar with the message of the movie that all emotions, even ones we perceive as negative, are important to our overall well-being and have a role in living a full life. One scene in that film always strikes me: Anxiety and Joy are in a battle for Riley's "command center," or decision-making area of her mind. As Joy tries to pry Anxiety away, Anxiety says, "I was just trying to protect Riley!"

Anxiety, though it has the best intentions to protect us,

doesn't make room for any other emotions, like joy, when it is given control and able to call all the shots. On Date Five, when you recognize your attachment patterns and emotions, like fear and anxiety, that want to take control of your dating life, it's important to acknowledge that all these emotions are a natural part of the process but you don't need to let fear or anxiety be in the driver's seat anymore. It can still, of course, be in the car, and you can listen to what it has to say, but fear doesn't make the final call.

You don't need to try to develop a new attachment style to find love. But you also don't need your attachment style to dictate the decisions you make on Date Five. The goal instead is to recognize your attachment style, give it voice, and understand what it's telling you about your past and the way you're wired and how that informs your approach to dating and finding love.

Strategy

Context + Conversation + Compatibility = Secure Attachment Loading

From a strategy standpoint, Date Five is where we transition into what I call the "contextuation date." It's a combination of a conversation date and a context date, while paying attention to compatibility. It's finally time to extend the length of the date and truly understand what it feels like to spend a significant amount of time with the other person—ideally at least half the day.

On Date Five, you need to understand this important nuance: You likely know if you have fun with this person and enjoy their company. You also hopefully know at this point that you can have deeper and more significant conversations with them. One green flag you should be looking for that is often disregarded is how seamlessly you can move between the serious and the silly aspects of life.

I've seen many couples who bonded over one or the other, the fun or the deep, only to discover in marriage that they can't move between the two so seamlessly. This disconnect ends up creating a feeling of loneliness as they navigate the vicissitudes of life together. Life is lived in the in-between. It's trying to have a serious conversation about feeling triggered at a family gathering and turning around to laugh at your dog who's scared of the vacuum cleaner. It's discussing a tough decision at work, acting as a sounding board for each other, and then asking in the next breath, "Do we have eggs at home, or should I pick some up at the store?"

We are complex beings with various layers, but on Date Five you should focus on this question: Can I see myself living *life* with this person? The mundane *and* the extraordinary? Often dating lends itself to deeper conversations that create emotional intimacy, especially in long-distance relationships. I've worked with many people who have experienced long-distance relationships not working out for the very reason that all they had bonded over was the serious stuff. When it came down to living in the same city, they realized they didn't enjoy the mundane and normal conversations. They didn't have the compatibility and attachment they needed to sustain the relationship.

What Most of Us Get Wrong

We often think that attachment styles don't change, but that's where we get it wrong. Even if you had the best parents and your attachment style has consistently been secure, you will tend to lean toward a more insecure attachment style when, for whatever reason, a relationship feels disconnected, uncertain, or distressed. The opposite is also true. Even if you had an insecure attachment as a child, your attachment style will become more secure if you're in a happy, romantic relationship.

People often ask me, "How can I become more secure in my attachment style when I'm single?" The answer? It's complicated. You can do all the work you want in therapy, but until you are in the ring, getting triggered and putting all that hard work to the test, you won't know if you're more secure.

This is one of the reasons I hold the controversial opinion that people wait far too long after a breakup to start dating again. We are often waiting for an "end point" to our healing because we don't realize that healing is a continuous journey, and secure attachment is also a lifelong journey, not a destination we ever fully arrive at. There are times when you may feel insecure, even in the most secure relationships. Your goal shouldn't be to live in a constant state of security because that's impossible. Instead, it should be secure attachment in your relationship that you can recalibrate to when life circumstances and disconnection create inevitable insecurity.

This is why I encourage getting out there in the dating

ring and not waiting for "complete healing" or waiting to be completely over your ex—or over any past relationship trauma. If that is the case, you could be waiting forever! Instead, what I recommend is dating with support. Getting the support of a therapist or dating coach helps you heal as you go instead of waiting for some arbitrary sign that you're "ready."

In love, as in life, it's easy to sit on the sidelines and be the critic. It's easy to think you see all the red flags and know all the reasons it won't work out with the person behind a two-dimensional dating app profile. It's easy to see all the flaws in your friend's boyfriend and think, "Man, I'm so happy I'm single!"

Do you know what's hard and brave? Being on the playing field. Swiping day after day, rejection after rejection, heartbreak after heartbreak, and still giving love a chance. As the famous "love chapter" of the Bible says, "Love never gives up" (1 Corinthians 13:7 NLT). So if love never gives up, why do we constantly give up on it? The answer, in short, usually comes down to our attachment style. We've created our understanding of love from an early age, and those have followed us into adulthood, into our dating experiences, and straight into Date Five, which is the turning point for many.

In your journey, Date Five may be the climax of the story for you. This may be the point when you decide if you'll continue or if you'll turn around. In every love story, there's a moment of decision: Will you choose to stay? If you've realized that anxiety or avoidance has taken control, I hope you finally take back the wheel and invite some joy and love to come in.

Don't Let Fantasy Have the Final Say

Many of us mistakenly believe we have a secure attachment style because we've never been "in the ring." This was the case for my client Haley. When she started working with me, she shared quite openly that she had very little experience dating. She grew up in a culture and faith-based community that believed only in courtship, a highly chaperoned form of getting to know someone that carried the high-pressure expectation that it would lead to marriage.

Because of her sheltered upbringing, Haley was confused when it came to finding love. She felt she had to learn right away if someone was a good fit for her or not, and she didn't allow most guys to get past Date One (or even get to Date One).

Wanting to know from the get-go isn't always a bad thing, but it can create a bit of an avoidant attachment that masquerades as secure by implying that you "know yourself well enough to know it's not going to work out." Sure, you might have looked at Haley's dating choices and thought she was simply clear on the kind of person she wanted, but the reality was that Haley wasn't giving *anybody* a chance. In fact, she wasn't even giving anybody a chance for her to *give* them a chance. She felt like she knew herself well enough to know when she didn't like how a guy laughed, or to trust when she "got the ick" after hearing his voice over the phone. I told her that we often self-sabotage by finding an excuse about why someone isn't the right fit for us.

"How do I know the difference between self-sabotaging

and my gut telling me a person isn't right?" she asked me during one session.

I explained to her that she had to get clarity on what she was looking for and not let her feelings or protective mechanisms be the CEO of her dating life. We decided that if someone met her main criteria—they were a practicing Christian, they had a stable job, and she felt attracted to them—then she'd be open to seeing where things went.

Nervous but excited, Haley moved forward in the dating process. Everything was feeling surprisingly effortless and easy with a guy named Joshua. That is, until sneaky Date Five came along. After the date, Haley showed up to our next session disappointed and confused.

"He's not the one," she told me.

I asked her what had happened and why she felt that way.

She responded, "I don't know. I had my first kiss *ever* last night, and it was so sweet and respectful. But afterward I had a nagging feeling that it's *not* right, he's not the one. I expected to feel different after my first kiss."

"How did you expect to feel?" I asked.

She sighed. "I expected to feel butterflies and sparks and fireworks."

"And how *did* you feel?" I probed.

"Well, it felt nice, but it felt . . . peaceful."

Now, before you balk at Haley's innocence and naivety, remember this: We all allow our attachment style to create an idea about a relationship or experience we imagine we will have, and when it doesn't meet our expectations—which are often based in fantasy, not reality—we immediately want to disconnect and protect ourselves. Behavioral psychologists call this the "fight or flight" response. When we feel potential threat or uncertainty, our primal response is either to "fight" and engage or to "fly" from the situation.

I knew that Haley's inexperience was in fact self-sabotage because she was comparing her reality to a fantasy. She couldn't tell me exactly why it felt wrong, because she'd never felt anything different. Her pattern was her preference. Her avoidant attachment style, fueled by her cultural beliefs about courtship, became the blueprint for her relationships. When her relationship with Joshua didn't align with this blueprint, it was so uncomfortable and unfamiliar that she wanted to run from it.

I was able to bring Haley back to reality by reminding her of the core criteria she was looking for and helping her distinguish her feelings (which were triggered by a fantasy in her head) from the facts. The assessment we conducted after each date also helped to ground her in reality.

Tools

Facts versus Feelings Assessment

This assessment is a great tool to use when distinguishing between facts and feelings. First, assess whether a change in your feelings is due to something your date *did*. Second, if they *did* do something you disliked, dig deeper and ask yourself how that behavior measures up against your core values and criteria. Was this just part of being human, or were they displaying a character issue that is out of alignment with who you are? And finally, was this incident a fluke, or was it a progression of previous behavior?

Here's what this assessment looked like in Haley's situation:

- Did Joshua do anything that made you feel like you're not compatible?
- Did he show any characteristics that made him seem like he isn't the person you want to be with?
- Did he show up drastically different on Date Five than he did on Dates One through Four?

Haley answered no to all these questions, which confirmed what I suspected: She was allowing her fear of the unknown and her avoidant attachment style to send her into flight mode. I encouraged her to lean in and go on another date with Joshua to give her nervous system a new experience.

Haley agreed to push past her Date Five attachment triggers and give Joshua another chance. As she leaned further into connection, she was able to feel safer in the relationship and learned how to better determine when her feelings were coming from a place of fear. And she was able to meet those fearful feelings with compassion and understanding: *Of course you're afraid! You want to protect me.*

Her fear hadn't been allowing her to create the life she wanted. And if she kept letting fear have control, it would ruin a potentially good relationship.

Haley is now in a happy relationship with Joshua where she can honor her desires and learn to feel secure in a relationship. I asked her recently if she ever ended up feeling the spark with Joshua, to which she replied, "I feel it daily in different ways. I realized that the spark isn't necessarily a moment; it's more like a general feeling I get when I think of him. It's less like a firework and more like a warm glow."

Her analogy was spot on. You see, friend, we often expect a spark to appear suddenly like a singular firework, a sign and confirmation that we should move forward in the relationship. If we haven't felt it by Date Five, we think we never will. What we don't realize is that sometimes we don't even know what we hope to feel, and we self-sabotage because of our insecurities. We do this when we allow our feelings to make decisions in isolation and *react* rather than *reflect* on the connection, person, and relationship as a whole.

Criteria Sandwich

Many people consider the checklist of what they're looking for in a person only *before* they find that person. The criteria sandwich truly comes in handy when you're in an attachment-based trigger zone between meeting someone and making the decision that they're your person. This is the way that I teach clients to think about their criteria for a potential partner. Essentially, the criteria sandwich involves recognizing that not all criteria are weighted equally. To build your sandwich, start with the bottom bun:

- **Bottom-bun criteria** are your "can't-haves," or deal-breakers, so there should only be a few, such as they can't smoke or do drugs. It's something they *do* have or do that you *don't* want.

- **Middle criteria** are the "like-to-haves"—wants, not needs—such as they share your taste in music, they love to read, etc. You can have as many of these as you want.
- **Top-bun criteria** are your must-haves, or your core criteria, such as they have a stable career, they share your faith, they want kids, etc. It's something they *must* have that you *do* want.

A common mistake people make in creating their criteria sandwich is choosing intangible qualities that I call "givens" (kind, loyal, etc.). Many of these criteria are qualities that *all* people should have. Another mistake is including criteria that you won't learn for a long time. The best criteria sandwich includes criteria that you can learn about quickly within the first five dates, letting you know if the person aligns with what you're looking for. It helps you slow down in order to speed up the process of building trust and security in a relationship.

After you've gone on Date Five and evaluated your attachment style and built your criteria sandwich, ask yourself:

1. Does this person still meet the main criteria I'm looking for in a partner?
2. Did they do anything or reveal anything that is a deal-breaker or red flag for me?
3. Has the general direction and progression of the dates been positive (each date gets better, not worse)?

If you answered yes to all these questions, it's time to move past this period of fear, recognize your avoidance, and lean in to determine if this person is a good fit.

Coaching Corner

The date: Like Date Four, Date Five is a "contextuation" date, a combination of conversation and context.

Ideal amount of time: 3–5 hours

Ideal settings: "Contextuation" dates may include dinner and a museum, a hike and a picnic, a cooking class and antique shopping, jet skiing and beach time.

Dos: Pay attention to your attachment tendency: Are you getting anxious about the connection and starting to worry about it not working out? Or are you starting to be hypercritical of the other person to protect yourself from vulnerability?

Don'ts: Don't push yourself or your date to define your connection yet. You still have some important information to gather about your date.

Questions to Ask on Date Five

- Tell me more about your childhood. Who was your favorite teacher and why?
- When you were a kid, what career did you think you wanted to have when you grew up?
- What was the hardest thing about launching into adulthood? What was the easiest?
- How has your relationship with your parents changed between childhood and adulthood?

Post-Date Five Reflections

• How am I feeling after Date Five? Has anything changed, and can I attribute that change to my attachment style?

• How is my attachment style impacting how I feel about my date?

• What are some attachment patterns from previous relationships that I want to change? What are some ways I can grow?

• Do I have too many deal-breakers? Too few? Should some of my deal-breakers actually be nice-to-haves? Does this person meet at least some of my nice-to-haves?

On Date Five, don't make a decision based on pure feeling or intuition or because you're waiting for a fireworks moment. Make sure you pause and reflect on the connection thus far, with the awareness that your desire and pattern for attachment may influence your decision to move forward or pull the plug. If you feel the need to pull the plug, make sure it's genuinely because of something your date is showing you. If you're not sure, always give it another date. Doing so doesn't mean you're saying yes to a marriage proposal; you're merely gaining more information.

DATE SIX

Red Flag or Carnival?

"Is it really a red flag? Because I'm starting to believe I'm color-blind!" Kendall said during one of our sessions. Most singles ask some version of this question around Date Six: "Is that a red flag or a carnival up ahead?" "Is it a light at the end of the tunnel or a train coming toward me?" A "red flag" was a wartime signal to the military that the enemy was incoming. They didn't toss up a red flag because they *thought* an enemy would show up. A red flag meant there was true, immediate danger.[1]

I told Kendall, "As popular as the term *red flag* has become, when it comes to dating, at times it can be difficult to decipher the difference between a true red flag and a flaw that may simply be an unfortunate side effect of belonging to the human race." We're pretty casual with our use of the term *red flag* today. It can mean everything from someone who has significant anger issues to someone who isn't quite as handy around the house as we would prefer.

For Kendall, on Date Six, she realized she liked James so much that she was willing to throw some blue paint on anything that even vaguely looked like a red flag and call it purple. For her own peace of mind, she needed the extended time of a contextuation date to assess whether she was seeing James clearly or through rose-colored glasses. She needed to dig deep into potential flaws and ask, "Am I being too accepting or hypercritical? Am I balancing the truth with grace?"

That's why it was important to be clear about whether James had legitimate red flags that revealed he wasn't a good fit for Kendall or if they were simply her own biases, which could be based on her own history, preferences, traumas, and unrealistic fantasies.

Flags Will Fly

You know those commercials for prescription medication—the ones with the laundry list of side effects at the end? Those side effects they speed through in the last fifteen seconds often seem a lot worse than the original symptom. Even if I might have been tempted to take the meds, by the end I think, "My problem isn't too bad. I think I'll live with it and not have to deal with those horrific side effects."

You may feel like that about relationships. This person in front of you is full of flaws, flags (of many colors), and fears. As you consider the possibility of marriage, the negative side effects may seem to far outweigh the potential benefits.

Cue the voiceover: "Relationship side effects may include, but are not limited to, complicated family dynamics, a long list of previous relationship failures, unusual devotion to the Kansas City Chiefs, a problematic best friend who plays video games all day, potential mental health struggles, financial instability, lack of ambition, and a delusion that they may make the roster of a professional baseball team someday."

Even the best medications have side effects. And even the most incredible humans have flaws and potential red flags. It's all about understanding which imperfections can be worked through or accepted and which ones aren't worth enduring.

In our increasingly polarized world, whether it comes to someone's politics or faith background or denomination, we as a society are increasingly eager to label, categorize, and stereotype other people.

Don't believe me? Let's try this experiment. I'll list some characteristics that are sometimes red flags in a dating relationship. After each of these words, think of a phrase or feeling that was triggered in you:

Divorced.
Unemployed.
Depressed.

Now, what if I told you that the man is divorced because his wife left him? He did his best to reconcile, but she refused, so he really didn't have a choice.

Still a red flag?

What if I said the unemployed guy just sold his multimillion-dollar company and is seeking his next business venture but is technically unemployed while he travels the world doing charitable work?

Still wouldn't give him a chance?

What if I told you the depressed man just lost his parent?

If he *wasn't* struggling with depression during that period of grief, you'd probably consider *that* a red flag.

We tend to see people either through rose-colored glasses or as red flags.

The truth is that some issues in relationships are less red than we think. In many ways it would be a whole lot more convenient if we could distinguish red flags like girls can distinguish the shades of nail polish—you know, the true OPI Red versus the Red Velvet Cupcake red. Usually, though, people and their issues more closely resemble shades of gray. Nobody is "all good" or "all bad," which makes it challenging for us to truly understand if they're relationship material.

On Date Six, the desire to label someone as a walking red flag at the first hint of an issue comes from our desire to protect more than our desire to connect. The irony is that both protecting and connecting are core to our survival, but we might not have the neural pathway to differentiate a romantic connection from a threat. When risk and reward are combined, all our brain sees is the risk, because it's trying to protect us. So when a potential romantic connection comes along and we see a potential red flag, guess what happens? All we feel is fear. All we can see is a threat, rather than seeing the whole picture.

Yes, there is risk in romance, but it is mild compared to the potential reward. Sometimes I wish we could comfort our nervous systems with the Scripture that says, "Our present sufferings are not worth comparing with the glory that will be revealed in us" (Romans 8:18).

Friend, the fear of potential suffering that pops up around Date Six, when you're assessing red flags, is nothing compared to the joy you will feel in a relationship where you choose to look beyond the flag color and see the fellow human next to you—yearning to be loved, longing to give love in return.

Painting Your Own Flags White

As my—and the rest of the world's—favorite artist of all time, Taylor Swift, sings in her Grammy Award–winning hit "Anti-Hero," "It's me, hi, I'm the problem, it's me."

Right now, you may be reading this chapter thinking, "Am I the problem? Do I have the red flags? This sounds an awful lot like my struggles."

As I reminded Claire when she wondered whether she was "fully healed" from the trauma of her past relationship to enter a new relationship with Preston, we *all* have red flags (or if you're being easy on yourself, burnt orange that in certain light can look red), whether we want to believe it or not.

I always recommend you look for the best possible fit for yourself while being the best possible version of yourself. This doesn't mean you're putting on a show or hiding the dynamics and challenges in your life. The way to be the best version of yourself is to assess your own risk factors and then identify or build in protective factors that can help buffer any potential negative side effects. Not quite sure how to do this? Here are some questions to get you thinking:

- Do I have any self-destructive or self-sabotaging behaviors?
- Do I have any qualities I would consider "red flags" if I saw them in someone else?
- How can I work on these qualities?
- Who can help me work on these qualities?
- Are any of these attributes things I can change, or are they part of who I am?

From my perspective, after working with thousands of singles navigating modern dating, I think this hyperpolarized world has made us quite—how do I put this kindly?— judgmental of the person next to us (or across from us on a date) and far less willing to identify the work we need to do on ourselves.

Now, I'll be the first person to tell you it's easy to say, "There are no good options out there," or "Every guy I meet has something wrong with him." But there's an elephant in the room that no one is talking about: *Of course* they have something wrong with them.

Unless you're reading this in a time when we're now dating across planet lines, you're looking to date a card-carrying member of the human race, and I hate to break it to you, but we're all far from perfect.

In my training as a couples therapist, I had to realize that instead of treating both people in the session individually, I essentially had to imagine *the relationship* as a third entity in the room. My client isn't one spouse or the other; my client is the relationship.

When you're on Date Six, I want you to think about

the other person's potential risk factors or red flags—not to evaluate how they affect you or make you feel, but rather how they would affect the type of *relationship* you want to build. On Date Six you're trying to get a clearer picture of your date through extended time with them. You'll need to remember details on Dates One through Five that caused a pause or created questions that require deeper digging. When you're on Date Six, the "context" piece of the date (for example, if you're taking a day trip to the beach) will help lighten the deeper conversations that you will aim to have to clarify any potential red flags. As you get to know this person in a deeper way, building on what you know from Dates One through Five, you'll be able to notice not only *what* they say but *how* they say it and whether they are aware of issues that could affect the relationship. This will help you think about the potential flaws as well as the potential gifts that contribute to this third entity: the relationship.

Think of the relationship like a plant you're growing in the garden. Maybe you go a bit heavy on the watering, which brings the plant down, but you're sensitive to giving it the correct amount of sunlight, which helps it. Your potential partner may be consistent with the watering, but they tend to buy the wrong soil; however, they can course-correct quickly.

On Date Six, you want to start seeing your date as a potential life partner with whom you grow toward a shared goal. Up until this point, you may have been viewing them through the lens of "Could this guy be 'the one'?" Now I want you to pivot and start asking yourself some new questions: "If I were with this person, what would our life together look like? What strengths would he bring to our future family?

What weaknesses would he need to work through? What is the shared vision we want to build together?"

You should transition from trying to see if you like this person to seeing if you can build something you like *with* this person. In this transition, you discover the unique beauty and vulnerability of our humanness. You learn to accept flaws with grace, understand true red flags, handle deal-breakers with compassion when the relationship can't move forward, navigate your own imperfections with care, and express the "truth in love" that the Bible talks about (Ephesians 4:15) so that you can grow.

In modern dating, sometimes we're so hyperfocused on someone else's flaws, red flags, love-bombing, ghosting, or any other buzzword we've created to explain bad behavior that we somehow lose sight of the opportunity to grow in our own areas of weakness.

 **Strategy**

Spot the Shade of Red

I like to separate red flags into two categories: relationship red flags and related red flags.

Relationship red flags are those that would make a person a bad match for *anyone*, not just a bad match for you. For example, if someone struggles with a severe mental illness that has been untreated, like antisocial personality disorder or narcissistic personality disorder, they are a bad match for anyone. They don't have the ability to be in a healthy relationship, no matter how mentally stable or capable of "dealing with them" a potential partner may be. Someone with those kinds of struggles is unable to connect with someone and meet another person's needs in a truly authentic way.

Related red flags, on the other hand, are the red flags someone has that are red only to *you*. Others may not find these red flags quite so problematic. For example, if you tend to be highly anxiously attached and insecure, someone who is avoidantly attached would not be a good match for you. Or if living close to your family is a core value to you, and the person you've been dating doesn't like the idea of living close to family, it's a red flag for you, even though the topic itself is neutral.

A Tale of Two Red Flags

Melissa was having a difficult time navigating the difference between a relationship red flag and a related red flag with David, the guy she was dating. He was everything she was looking for in many ways, but after Date Five, he started talking more openly about his parents' relationship and his family dynamics.

David grew up in a family that looked similar to Melissa's from the outside: His parents were traditional, had been married for many years, and didn't believe in divorce. They were committed to their faith and culture. Melissa considered this to be a positive—it seemed like David's family and hers shared many similarities.

However, Melissa's parents had a loving and connected relationship, while David's family dynamic was a bit more complex and less healthy. During Date Six, while they were browsing antiques and grabbing home-baked pastries at a small-town bakery nearby, David reminisced about growing up in a similar small town and mentioned that walking through town with his parents was sometimes an uncomfortable experience. He told Melissa about one time when his dad got mad at his mom for purchasing an antique item he viewed as too expensive. David shared how embarrassed he was by how his dad spoke to his mom in public. This vulnerable moment allowed Melissa to assess more deeply a potential red flag David had brought up earlier in their dating journey: his parents' relationship.

Melissa was careful to tread lightly, saying, "That must have been challenging to navigate feeling embarrassed but also not being able to stand up to him as a young boy." She dealt with the topic sensitively, without asking direct questions, but instead stating an observation that invited him to share more.

David said his dad often spoke negatively about his mom and didn't show her the love and care that were indicative of a healthy relationship. They stayed together, but mostly because of appearances, shared values, and the kids.

While David appeared to be aware that his parents' dynamic wasn't ideal, he also seemed to admire his dad in many ways and considered him to be a good family man for working hard and providing. Melissa's definition of a good family man was very different, because though her dad likewise worked hard and provided for their family, he also respected her mom and showed immense love to her.

At this point in the relationship, Melissa was confused.

Was this a red flag? How much had David's parents' example affected how he would act as a husband and father? Should his less-than-ideal upbringing be considered a mark against him? Was it a generational pattern he could overcome, or was he prone to repeat the cycle?

Melissa had many valid questions when she came to speak with me about this dilemma. She felt that they had a great connection and that David checked all the boxes of what she was looking for in a partner—at least on paper. But Melissa genuinely wanted to have a family, and choosing an emotionally healthy partner to be the father of her future children was a huge priority. She knew the importance of the role and example of a father, and discovering more about the dynamics in David's family had made her nervous. Could she find someone with all the qualities David had, the great connection they had, *and* parents who portrayed a healthy example of marriage?

As Melissa processed her thoughts out loud, I knew part of her was looking for guidance and part of her was afraid of what I was going to say. The truth is, she wasn't wrong to be concerned. But, as always, there was more to the story that Melissa needed to uncover.

Is the Risk Greater than the Reward?

Research shows us that although unhealthy relationship dynamics between parents do negatively affect their children, they don't necessarily cause the pattern to repeat. Instead, this is what we would call a "risk factor"—something that could be potentially damaging but also could be balanced out if enough "protective factors" are involved.[2] Protective factors are positive aspects or traits of a person that help them deal more effectively with stress and the challenges that their risk factors may create for their overall well-being.

I dug a little deeper. "Did David have any other positive role models in his life?" I asked.

"Yes," Melissa answered. "He spent a lot of time with his grandparents, and they were sweet and loving. He says he felt more attached to his grandfather than his own father."

Check.

"Has he ever processed, or is he open to processing, with a therapist or counselor what he witnessed and experienced in his family dynamic growing up?" I continued.

"Actually, he goes to a therapist regularly—and has been going to one since his teenage years. He also has an accountability group that he's been a part of for years."

Gold star to David!

"Did he have a good and supportive relationship with his siblings?"

"Yes, he says his brother is his best friend, and his sister often distracted them when their parents were fighting. They formed a close bond and developed resilience together, and it seems like they still stand up for, encourage, and protect one another."

Great! Research shows that sibling bonds can often buffer the potentially harmful effects of an unstable household.[3]

Everyone has "risk factors"—things that can potentially negatively affect a relationship. David, despite this risk factor, appeared to be doing his part to reverse a negative generational pattern. He had a healthy sense of awareness that his parents, though he loved them individually, didn't have a dynamic he wanted to emulate, and he was doing the work necessary to prevent repeating this pattern. He'd taken steps to process this in therapy, to seek out better role models in his grandparents, and to lean on other people for support (such as his siblings and accountability group). Learning these details on Date Six helped Melissa color in the lines of what she had learned about David thus far, with the right colored pencil, and no, it wasn't red.

Melissa was able to follow the trail of related red flags that marked legitimate concerns about David's family of origin. Before she moved forward with their relationship, she needed to know David was aware of how his parents' relationship affected him, had healthy relationships with other family members, and was dedicated to changing unhealthy dynamics.

On Date Six, many potential risk factors or red flags become clearer through extended time together on a "context and conversation" date that may look like a mini day trip to the touristy town a few hours away. This time together is when you need to make sure you're being alert, informed, and discerning. You've worked through the potential self-sabotage that can happen on Date Five when the insecure attachment style is triggered, and now it's time to understand and navigate the other person's humanity—imperfections, flaws, and all.

Put Me In, Coach!

Many of us daydream about what it would feel like to be in a relationship with someone who checks all the boxes and has no red flags. We want them to come from a great family background, be at least six feet tall, have an Ivy League diploma, and look like they walked out of a magazine cover. But will that person laugh at your weird jokes while you're burning dinner? Will they listen to you crying over a friendship breakup you never saw coming? Will they talk you through a tough meeting with your boss, support you, and be on your side (even if you made a mistake or were in the wrong)?

These are the real moments of life, the ones in which we want and need love.

By Date Six, we can find ourselves looking for flaws and hyperfocusing on risk factors in an effort to protect ourselves. As they say, "A good offense is the best defense." But when we do this, we don't always see the reality: We also bring some risk factors to the relationship.

One of my favorite parts of the Bible is in 1 Samuel when God chose a very unlikely someone to be ruler of Israel. He didn't have the accolades, the appearance, or anything else that would have made him the number one choice. But God sees beyond what we typically see. "The LORD said to Samuel, 'Do not consider his appearance or his height, for I have rejected him. The LORD does not look at the things people look at. People look at the outward appearance, but the LORD looks at the heart" (1 Samuel 16:7).

Don't get me wrong—there are true red flags, and often they mean that the relationship isn't the right fit. But sometimes we must flip the script when it comes to decision-making. We have to peek behind the layers, beyond the potential red flags, and truly look at the heart.

Parting the Red Flag Sea

Date Six is what I think of as the parting of the Red Sea—a sea of red flags, that is. You need to channel your inner Moses and part the Red Sea to find out if there's dry land beneath all the butterflies, the risks, the compliments, and the confusion. The bottom line is, going into this date, you need to be aware of one supreme measure that people use to hide red flags: *love-bombing*. If you've been love-bombed up until this point without knowing it, Date Six is where I want you to look beyond the gifts, the phone calls, the grand statements about the future, and the thoughts of how attractive your future children will be.

If you're noticing that the fantasy this person has painted isn't matching reality, you might be a victim of love-bombing.

Love-bombing is when one person in a dating relationship showers the other with compliments, gifts, and attention in an extreme and manipulative way to get the person to attach and feel like they're falling in love when they're actually just "bombed" so much that they can't see past the smoke and mirrors. This experience makes it more challenging to see the red flags that typically pop up around now, because the love-bombed partner has become emotionally attached too quickly.

The key here is to avoid getting emotionally attached until you have more information about the other person— and definitely not waiting until Date Ten to have a mature, real, honest conversation about starting a relationship. If love-bombing is afoot, you may be getting a lot of pressure to seal the deal now, rather than go through the prescribed ten dates. What can you do here at Date Six to be both open-minded to a possible relationship with this person while also keeping some important emotional gates up?

In our Western society, we expect our partner to fill the role of not only a spouse but also a best friend, business partner, and intellectual match who likes the same hobbies and books and never argues over the remote control or takes hours to decide what to watch on Netflix because you both enjoy all the same TV shows and movies. Am I right?

You may be rolling your eyes, but many people look for a spouse the same way they look for members for their book club. Where did this concept of love come from?

As an Armenian, I've asked many members of my community, including my parents and grandparents, how they met their spouse. The answer I get is quite different from the "how we met" story you may hear from your coworker or see in the credits of *Sleepless in Seattle*.

Love Takes a Village

In Western culture, many of us are effectively "villageless" in our social lives, our emotional lives, and our actual lifestyle. We're independent, to a fault. If I were to diagnose American society, I'd say it was avoidantly attached. If Western dating were a person, it would be Leonardo DiCaprio.

Dating itself is a Western construct. Up until the 1900s, marriage was seen more as a business transaction than a choice built on love. In most cultures, marriages were arranged through families or through a matchmaker.

Online dating is even more recent, since the 2000s, and

has grown more popular and lost much of its stigma in the last ten years.

Because of the hyperindependence of American society and the desire to "do it our own way," we've created the process of dating but haven't truly taken the time to learn *how* to date. We assume it will come naturally, but it hasn't been socialized in us or taught to us because the generations before us were the beta testers, still trying to figure it out themselves.

Why am I giving you a mini history of dating as we process Date Six? Because up until this point, you may have had the idea that your dates are all fun and games until someone gets hurt. And now that you've learned about some risk factors and potential red flags, you may be worried that the person about to get hurt by this modern made-up construct of dating is you!

Tools

Phone a Friend

It's around Date Six that I recommend calling for reinforcements. Bring in a trusted friend who can help you differentiate between love-bombing and genuine interest. Are there red flags that this friend can see because they're not blinded by the love potion that may have taken effect on Dates One through Five? A trusted friend can offer their observations and help you sort through any confusion you feel. After all, it's great to be going on dates with someone who is thoughtful, brings you flowers, and shows genuine interest in you. But the line between thoughtful gestures and love-bombing can be thin. Another set of trusted eyes can help you discern what's going on.

Like in an episode of *Who Wants to Be a Millionaire*, I am introducing the phone-a-friend lifeline at Date Six and not any sooner, because it's important to learn how to trust yourself in the dating process and not always outsource your decisions. You don't want to use a lifeline until it's absolutely necessary. When you're looking for love, you want the process to be truly *yours*. You want to make the choices that are best for you, but you also don't want to feel the crushing weight of your decisions without the support of your village.

Like in *Who Wants to Be a Millionaire*, the friend you call shouldn't necessarily be your best friend or your most optimistic friend. It should be the friend you think of as most knowledgeable in general about these situations, through either learned or lived experience, who can lovingly speak the truth to you. On the show, the contestant has to choose which friend they're going to call *before* they know what question they're going to be stumped on, and I recommend you do the same. Resist calling the friend who will give you the feedback you want to hear. Instead, call the friend who will deliver the truth so you can make the best decision for *you*.

With a Little Help from My Friends

It may feel like it's just you and your choices, but if possible, meet up with a trusted friend for part of Date Six—and maybe with one of your date's friends. Bringing your date into your community—and their community into yours—may be just what you need for this relationship to grow and blossom.

Part of developing a feeling of safety in a potential relationship is being around others who make you feel safe and noticing whether this person makes you feel the same way. At the risk of aging myself, as some of my favorite philosophers of the 1990s, the Spice Girls, would say, "If you wanna be my lover, you gotta get with my friends."[4]

If you have a kind and caring community, if you've found "your people," if you have friends who affirm you and encourage you, you can rest assured that when you introduce them to your date, one of two things will happen. If your date doesn't match the high standard of the people you've already created healthy relationships with, they will stick out like a sore thumb and they won't last. If they *do* match that standard, you know you've found a relationship with the potential to last.

Say No to Negativity Bias

Another reason you need to bring in friends to help you assess your date is because of *negativity bias*. This is a psychological phenomenon in which our brain is biased toward negative thinking, which leads us to emphasize red flags and potential incompatibilities and flaws rather than focusing on our potential partner's positive qualities.

Negativity bias is why we can get all As except for that one A- on a report card, but we beat ourselves up about the A-.

In dating, this is often why we feel the need to prove ourselves, and why we focus on the one person who doesn't like us, despite there being plenty of people who *do* want to date us. That reminds me of an internet meme I once saw that showed a single girl on her knees praying, "Please, send me my husband!" When God sends her someone, she responds, "Not that one—he's five foot nine!"

If I could guess, I'd say God wasn't amused.

Psychologically speaking, negativity bias serves us when we're able to perceive a threat and avoid it. We can be hypervigilant when necessary and not let anything—or anyone—hurt us. When it comes to dating and learning if someone could be the right fit, we tend to turn up the volume on our internal negativity bias the more we get to know someone, because the potential for someone to break our heart increases as we give more of our heart away.

If you're an Avoidant Ava, as discussed in Date Five, you've already been looking for a way to avoid vulnerability, so if your date made it this far, that feeling has carried over into this date. The flaws you noticed but felt like you could get over are now amplified during Date Six because of negativity bias.

You might also be facing the paradox of choice, like we talked about in Date One. "This person is great," we might think, "but can I find someone *better*?" The "grass is greener" mindset is a form of negativity bias that sabotages our ability to be content with an amazing potential partner who, albeit, is still human.

So how do we overcome negativity bias and not let it sabotage our potential relationship? The first way, as mentioned earlier, is by inviting friends and family, a trusted advisor, a therapist, or an expert into the Negative Town in your mind. Just because it's there doesn't mean you have to live there. Allowing someone you trust to give you honest feedback about your thoughts on potential flaws in a partner is important. And by the way, make sure you take *their* biases into consideration as well before you take their advice.

If you have a friend who tends to be superficial in the type of guy she dates and won't go out with someone unless he looks like Brad Pitt—twenty years ago—then you know she's not the best person to give you an objective opinion when you're not sure you're 100 percent attracted to a person. If you ask the opinion of a mentor from church who's been in a loving and committed marriage for forty-plus years, she'll offer a more objective and helpful perspective.

In summary, Date Six is all about spotting red flags: Is this person a good fit for a relationship in general? Are they a good fit for you personally? Did you receive feedback from friends that warrants a pause?

Coaching Corner

The date: A half-day trip to a nearby tourist town

Ideal amount of time: Up to half a day

Ideal settings: Beach or mountain trip, exploring and shopping in a tourist town, music festival (long breaks and opportunity for conversation)—something with potential to meet up with a friend for a portion of the date (maybe they live in the town you're visiting).

Dos: Pay attention to the positives, even within difficult stories. How is this person turning their "weakness" into a strength? Allow a trusted friend to weigh in, and thoughtfully consider their perspective while still honoring your own wisdom.

Don'ts: Don't try to paint the red flags you're seeing a different color, and don't forget that you yourself have red flags.

Questions to Ask on Date Six

- What is something you've struggled with?
- If you could change one thing about yourself, what would it be?
- Who would you consider to be your community? What role do they play in your life?
- Have you ever lost someone or something important to you? How did you process the grief?

Post-Date Six Reflections

- If I were with this person, what would our life together look like?
- What strengths would they bring to our future family?
- What weaknesses would they have to work through?
- What was I hoping my friend would say about this person? How did I feel about their actual feedback?

Even the healthiest and happiest relationships consist of two people with their own shade of red flags—hopefully it's more of a burnt orange. But on Date Six it's exciting to learn about how someone has grown on their journey. Now is the time to see how the resilience and character they've built could make them a great copilot for you!

DATE SEVEN

Setting the Stage for Commitment

"How can I be sure I'm ready to be in a relationship with him?" This was the text I got from Carly before her Date Seven with Matt. Like all of us, Carly wanted certainty before moving forward into commitment. She had been hurt in the past, and even though she'd followed my advice up until this point, she still wanted to be sure she wasn't missing something before she fully let her guard down.

Have you ever walked into the wrong room at a movie theater and sat through the previews, only to realize it wasn't the movie you paid to see? If you're a megafan of *The Office* like me, you may remember the episode in season 2 when Pam, the secretary who's secretly in love with Jim the salesman, is chatting with Jim about how she rented the Sandra Bullock comedy-drama *28 Days*. She recounts to Jim that she kept watching and watching, waiting for Sandra to show up, but ultimately realized she hadn't been watching *28 Days* but rather *28 Days Later*, an apocalyptic horror movie. (Spoiler alert: Our girl Sandra is *not* saving the world in *28 Days Later*.)

As Jim laughs at Pam, he says, "No way! How did you confuse *28 Days* with *28 Days Later?*"

Pam defends herself, explaining, "I rented it from Blockbuster! They don't put pictures on the box!"[1]

Fair point, Pam. Fair point.

As much as we say not to judge a book by its cover, the scene in that episode reminds me of what happens for most people when Date Seven rolls around. In your previous dating experiences, you may have thought you were Drew Barrymore in *The Wedding Singer*, the main character in your very own romantic comedy, ready to find true love. But eventually you had a budding realization that you were Drew Barrymore in *Scream*, trying to dodge some dude's scary phone calls. What you thought was the beginning of a fairy-tale romance may have started to look—and feel—like a scary movie you wanted to escape from. "What even happened?" you wondered.

The answer: There were glimpses of hope and potential along the way that kept you wanting to see the ending. You were waiting for Sandra Bullock to pop out, even though the apocalypse you were watching was hinting that she probably wasn't coming!

This is exactly what Carly had experienced in the past and was now trying to avoid with Matt before Date Seven. Far too often, I've seen people initially agreeing on things in a general sense. They get emotionally attached, only to discover that while they thought they were on the same page regarding where the relationship was going, they were reading completely different books and in different languages!

Sometimes it looks like this: You know you're ready to have kids in the next couple of years, and you thought the person you're dating was too. But what they meant by "ready to have kids" was "Eventually, maybe I can see myself being a father—if you're willing to change every diaper and my life won't change or be inconvenienced at all." If biological fertility factors are affecting your timeline of having children, discovering that the person you're dating has a far different understanding of that timeline makes for a sobering dose of reality.

For some of my clients, like Carly, this disconnect has led to some discomfort, difficult conversations, and even breakups. The truth is, when you assess the deeper details behind the "cover," you're able to move on with a better sense of empowerment and focus. You're freed to find someone who wants the same things you do instead of falling for someone who isn't going to give you your happily ever after.

The Case against the Exceptional Love Story

Every once in a while, someone says to me, "But, Dr. Christie, my cousin fell in love with someone on the first date, they got married a week later, and they've been married for thirty years and seem pretty happy!"

To which I say, congratulations to them and I wish them all the happiness! However, this is what I like to call the "exceptional" love story. Sure, it happens. But when it comes to love, in my opinion, it's miraculous enough if we find some-one with whom we genuinely want to spend the rest of our lives. We shouldn't require our love story to have all kinds of lightning-strike magic like we're auditioning for the next

Nicholas Sparks movie. Don't try to chase after the miracle story—chase the miracle itself: love.

There's always an exception to the rule, but the rule is the most likely outcome. While we love to hear the "exception" stories, we should desire to live the "rule" of life when it comes to determining whether someone is relationship material. Rules keep people safe, and in the game of hearts, you want to keep yours as safe as possible. Trust me, there will be excitement and exceptions in your life and love story, some of which you never could have imagined, some of which are better than you ever could have dreamed. But an exception-to-the-rule kind of love story doesn't make the love more valid. It doesn't make the love more special. And quite frankly, you shouldn't seek to be the exception to the rule.

Around Date Seven, many people are chomping at the bit to be "official." That's often because of the way they've typically experienced dating, instead of through this intentional ten-date process. In typical dating, as soon as there's a flutter of chemistry and compatibility, we're ready to stick a label on it and call it a day. Alert the press! We're official!

If you're tempted to do that after reading this book, remember, you've seen how that's worked out before. You made some kind of commitment, only to discover that all kinds of other pages were hidden beneath that front cover. The goal with this ten-date process is to keep pressing in, to learn as much as you can about the other person in a sequential, intentional way, so that when the time comes to determine the future of the relationship, you can do it with your head and your heart aligned.

This can feel like a radical shift away from how you've done things before. If you've been following the steps up to this point on each date, you likely know the person you've been going on dates with far better than you've ever known anyone else at this point in the dating process. You might be thinking, "Dr. Christie's way of dating works! I feel like I really know this person, and I'm ready to make if official!"

While I congratulate you on changing up the way you've dated and for tossing old patterns that didn't serve you, I want to encourage you to pretend you're on a ride at Disneyland and to "hold tight and stay seated with your seat belt fastened." You're not ready to get off the ride yet. If you do, you could get hurt. You need to continue to guard your heart and keep your hands open to whatever comes next, not focus on one specific outcome. Why? Because the next several dates— starting with Date Seven—are key to understanding what this person is about on a deep level.

As they say, seven is God's number, and it means "completion." After Date Six, hopefully you've learned a lot about the other person, you feel good around them, and you've had some deep conversations that make you feel confident to move forward. Now, during Date Seven, it's time to go deeper to confirm that what you've learned so far is accurate. You've done the work; now it's time to double-check it.

If you can recall from our conversation in Date Two, you may have had a desire to dive into the deep end of certain topics, but I told you that if you were patient, the right time and place to do so would arise.

Well, here we are. Date Seven is the time and place to take that deeper dive.

At this point, you're not simply receiving information on random family drama from someone you've known less than a week and trying to take that in and decide whether this person could be your future spouse. Instead, you've layered the process so that you've arrived at a place that feels organic and comfortable and enables you to see someone as a whole person, rather than making decisions based on bits and pieces of their story.

Carly had gotten to know Matt holistically, so I advised her to approach Date Seven with the focus of gaining clarity through deeper conversations. Carly opted for a romantic comedy with Matt followed by dinner, as I had suggested, to make the topic about relationships and finding love transition seamlessly while they ate. She was able to ask questions like, "That relationship mirrored some aspects of my past relationship, which reminded me of something you said about an ex not having similar goals. Would you be open to sharing more?" Her gentle queries allowed her to get clarity about this crucial area of past relationships before committing and to avoid a common mistake she had made in past relationships.

 **Soul Work**

Understanding the Economics of Commitment

Let's look at commitment from a different angle. In relationships, we see an experience that is similar to the way one

makes a financial investment. The sunk-cost fallacy in eco-
nomics refers to when someone is hesitant to abandon a
course of action because they've significantly invested in it.
Research finds that the more invested people are in relationships, the more committed they are, which is a result of
"commitment bias."[2] This is why we often stay in unhealthy
relationships. If we were to end them, all the time, energy,
and care we invested in the relationship would go to waste.
This is how Carly, and many other singles I've worked with,
have become stuck in the fear of uncertainty. They invest a
lot in a person, don't assess correctly whether they're aligned,
and by the time they discover they're not, they're too invested
and loyal to walk away.

When you make a commitment too early on in any
relationship, it could cause you to overlook things you previously would have considered a red flag or a deal-breaker.
That's commitment bias. Some research has even concluded
that investment is the strongest predictor of whether a
relationship will last but doesn't necessarily mean it will be a
happy relationship.[3]

So when you invest, be sure you're making an educated
investment. As the saying goes in the world of employment,
"Hire slow, fire fast." The reason behind this saying is that
people tend to hire too fast and wait too long for someone
to "prove themselves" or for things to get better but end up
losing money, time, and emotional energy in the process.
This is also good advice when it comes to this point in the
dating process. When a huge red flag or deal-breaker arises
before Date Ten and before you're emotionally invested, it's
much easier to say, "This isn't a fit," and stop the relationship

before it starts. If you notice those same deal-breakers and red flags too far into the investment, however, you will often try to make it work, even against your better judgment and to your own detriment.

This is why delaying emotional investment for as long as possible is key to ensuring that you come to understand the important things about a person *before* you've made an official commitment to them. On Date Seven, it's not about having all the answers. It's not about tying all the complex situations in someone's life into a pretty bow so you can be in a relationship with them. Date Seven is about *clarity*. That's what I want you to feel at the end of this date—that you have a clear sense of who this person is, the complexities they bring to the table, and what this means for the relationship you've imagined for yourself.

You want to know you've asked the questions you need answers to before moving forward toward a commitment while also recognizing that you won't know the whole story and more layers will be revealed over time. Clarity doesn't mean you have *all* the answers, but it does mean you've asked the questions and received the answers you need to be confident moving ahead into a potential relationship.

 **Strategy**

Clarity before Commitment

Singles need to assess several areas before they are ready for a committed relationship. The following areas help you fill in the blanks on someone's past, present, and future and make you feel confident to start a new chapter with them as your significant other.

Vision for the Future

As cliché as this sounds, asking the other person, "Where do you see yourself in five years?" is important. It gives you a good idea of what they want to spend their time doing, what their priorities will be in the near future, and what they want their legacy to be.

This conversation about the upcoming five years creates an important on-ramp to talk about finances. Many people delay this conversation even though research shows that finances are a top point of contention in relationships and one of the primary reasons for divorce.[4] Having the conversation about finances on Date Seven gives you clarity on your date's ideas about money and their current financial situation. You may have picked up on some of this in previous dates, but having a targeted conversation is important. Consider asking some of these questions:

- What are your thoughts and beliefs about money?
- Do you lean more toward saving or spending?
- What are your family's beliefs about money?
- Do you tend to be more generous or more frugal?
- What are your financial goals? For example, do you want to be a homeowner?
- What are your beliefs around finances and gender roles?
- What are your thoughts on budgeting?

- What is your salary range and your retirement plan?
- What do you spend your money on?
- Do you have any significant debt? If so, do you have a plan for paying it off? (When you listen to their response, note the difference between good debt—things like solid investments and student loans—and bad debt—things like frivolous purchases or risky investments.)

At this point, you should have built enough trust and vulnerability with this person to talk more deeply about this topic. If they aren't willing to talk about finances with you at this point, that's important to note. I would advise you not to formalize any relationship in which you don't have clarity about finances.

Core Values

It's important to get clarity on the core values that are essential to your date's identity and their lifestyle. If you're not sure, ask. But first be clear on what your own values are and then note if there are fundamental differences. Maybe a core value of theirs is a nomadic lifestyle and you are a dentist in private practice, needing to set deep roots in a community for your practice to thrive. This value discrepancy should make you pause before moving forward with the relationship. Are they willing to give up the nomad life to support your dental practice? Are you willing to give up your practice to follow them in that wanderlust life? Is there a compromise you're both willing to make?

Physical Intimacy

Here's where you're getting the tea! Maybe on an earlier date, your partner briefly mentioned their "problematic" ex. For some reason, you were a little skeptical. You hoped more details would come up naturally, but that hasn't happened and you have some further questions. You know you can't move forward without getting clarity in this area. This is the date to open that topic back up and get more details.

- Have you had any significant past relationships?
- Why did those relationships end?
- What were qualities your ex had that you felt were a good fit?
- What were qualities your ex had that you felt weren't a good fit?
- Were these relationships physically intimate?

Because of its delicate nature, many people make the mistake of not asking questions regarding sexual history while they're in the early stages of dating someone. If that hasn't been discussed, I think it's important to bring up either at this point or in the next date or two. As a Christian therapist, I've seen many clients across the spectrum with different beliefs, values, and standards around sex, and I recommend these conversations happen before you're in a committed relationship. Emotional and physical health are important components of someone's sexual history.

Historically in the Christian community, people have felt that sex education would lead to sex. Often in our faith communities, this belief has made us hesitant to talk with honesty about our physical bodies, the experience of sex, and education about both safe sex practices and sexual fulfillment. Of course, I believe there's an appropriate time and place for these conversations, but are you ready for this hot take? If you're a dating adult, the time is now. Knowing how someone's physical and sexual history affects your current relationship is very important.

And here's a nuance you don't often hear: It's also important to know how much you need to know and which details are better left unspoken.

The purpose of this conversation isn't to elicit fear or shame or to get all the details, but rather to understand how someone's values, history, and experiences shape who they are today and whether you should consider moving forward with them. It's a fine line to walk when it comes to knowing how exactly to ask questions and get information while still being respectful of someone's personal boundaries. Ideally at this point, this person has made you feel safe in various ways and has deemed themselves someone you can be vulnerable with, and vice versa. Sharing your own history, beliefs, and values is an important piece of navigating past relationships at this point as well.

When you're having this conversation, pay careful attention to how they respond to your questions. Suppose you lead off the conversation by saying, "There's no comfortable way to ask this question, but would you be open to sharing about your history with intimacy in past relationships?" And then notice *how* they answer the question. Are they honest? Defensive? Authentic? Do they minimize or deflect? Also pay attention to *what* they say, and make sure you're aware of your boundaries, deal-breakers, and preferences as they share their own history.

On upcoming dates, you're going to dive deeper into a couple of other topics that are incredibly important and can also feel a little intrusive. Remember, these are topics you must cover before you take the relationship to an official status. *You must gather this information in a deliberate, intentional process in order to decide if this person is right for you.* Skipping over these topics can be a recipe for disaster.

Love yourself well enough to gain the clarity you need.

Family Dynamics

Family dynamics can be a complex and sensitive area to explore. What is their family of origin like? What are their relationships like? Are they close or distant? What are some potential negative patterns they have? We'll dive into this more in Date Eight, but for now keep in mind that this area is one of the most influential indicators of how someone will show up in a relationship.

Mental Health Challenges

Whew, I'm going there. Yes, as a therapist, I believe it's *so* important that discussions of mental health challenges come up early and often. Maybe this person has struggled with mental health in the past. Maybe they will in the future. Where do they stand on getting help, whether they need more support now or later? What's their stance on couples therapy? It's my recommendation that if they currently do or ever have struggled with a severe form of mental illness, they need to be getting consistent help from a therapist, life coach, or spiritual director to prevent potential relapses.

These are some of the most important questions to ask and get clarity about. I've seen many a person devastated by the effects of an untreated mental health issue, and I don't want you to suffer the same fate. Recent research says that 21 percent of adults experience at least one mental illness, and 55 percent of those adults have not received any treatment. More concerning is the upward trend in recent years of more and more Americans struggling with mental health and increased distress.[5]

Not only does mental illness impact an individual's functioning and quality of life, but it also severely impacts relationships, with some studies citing that mental health disorders such as addiction, depression, and PTSD increase the risk of divorce up to 80 percent.[6]

I've worked with many people in couples therapy who either never knew about their spouse's struggle with mental health or addiction or had some level of denial and didn't see the warning signs. If you're reading this and saying, "I've been there," you may be feeling some level of guilt or shame that I want to release you from. Many people have entered a relationship and truly didn't see any red flags or signs, or maybe they saw some version of struggle but didn't realize the severity or were deceived to believe it wasn't that big of an issue.

No one is beyond the possibility of having a healthy and beautiful relationship. No matter your struggle or the struggle of the person you're dating, hope and help are available for everyone. The key at this point, on Date Seven, is to ask the question and develop the awareness.

Everyone has baggage. Everyone enters a relationship with various challenges and struggles. But you need to have open and honest conversations about these struggles so you are confident that this person can be your teammate, going in the same direction toward health in every area of life, not someone who is inflexible, unwilling to grow and work through challenges together.

The natural next question I get is, "Well, what if I ask the questions and they lie to me?"

Maybe this question is coming from experience. Maybe it's coming from fear. Unfortunately, sometimes you won't know someone is lying to you until you discover the truth.

I'm not suggesting that you take what someone says at face value. This is why we've been learning how to assess someone's character: by observing it over a period of time and in different contexts *before* you get emotionally attached.

Because you've been getting to know someone in this way, you can then ask direct questions about their life, their mental health, and their relationships. You can proceed with awareness. But remember this: Love always includes risk. There are no guarantees in love, as we discussed in Date Four. You're doing the best you can, and you have to entrust the rest to God.

Learning from Lainey's Journey

This is where Lainey found herself on Date Seven. She tended to be the anxious type and had struggled with codependency in past relationships, but she felt connected and safe with Dan.

When she and Dan got to Date Seven, she knew she had

some clarifying questions to ask, and she felt nervous about doing this. "What if it all falls apart?" she wondered.

I challenged her, asking, "What if having these honest conversations helps you relax in love and feel closer and safer than ever before?" (This wasn't my first rodeo, and I knew what would happen.)

She agreed, and what happened next surprised her, in a good way.

Dan shared that he had struggled with an addiction to alcoholism in his teens and early twenties and considered himself a "sober alcoholic." He'd been part of the Alcoholics Anonymous program for ten years, had a sponsor, and was in active recovery. He felt relieved and grateful that Lainey had opened up the conversation, because he'd wanted to discuss this very thing before he asked her to be his girlfriend.

When Lainey shared this information with me, I knew she was worried I was going to tell her to break up with Dan. And so I asked her, "How did you feel after he shared that with you?"

"Honestly, I felt surprised I wasn't more anxious," she told me. "I'd been so worried about this conversation that I almost felt relieved he opened up to me, and it gave me a lot of peace that he's working on himself every day, with the help of support from his community and church. That's more than many guys I've dated before! Do you think I should break up with him because of his past? He did say he has to take it one day at a time and treat every day like a new day to stay in recovery."

She then asked me, "Do you think this is a deal-breaker?"

When she and I looked back at her list, we saw that she had put as one of her deal-breakers "active and serious mental health issues."

Since Dan had been in recovery for a decade, it seemed he had a new lifestyle and way of being. He had a support plan and was working on himself.

"Well, it doesn't seem this fits your deal-breaker criteria," I told her, "since his addiction isn't what we would call active but rather in recovery. But it's important to get more clarity and write down a list of questions you have for him."

We worked together on some questions Lainey would ask Dan:

- Do you have any other mental health struggles?
- What are some of the triggers in your life?
- What do you do if you're having a hard day and feel like you want to drink?
- What would happen if you relapsed?

Once we felt good about her list of questions, I told Lainey that all *she* could do would be to take it one day at a time with this new awareness. She wasn't agreeing to a marriage proposal or even a relationship yet. She was seeking clarity on whether she wanted to move forward.

Dan's struggle with addiction didn't define him. And Lainey's struggle with anxiety and codependence didn't define her. If they both committed to working on themselves individually—and on the relationship when times got tough—they would be leaps and bounds ahead of many couples by taking that personal insight and creating a beautiful, intentional, and loving healthy relationship.

Sneak peek into the future happy ending: Lainey and Dan entered a committed relationship, got married, and are now counseling individuals in their church who also have struggled with addiction.

If you were in Lainey's shoes, would you have made the same decision? For you, it may be a deal-breaker if someone struggles with addiction at any point, of any kind. But here's something to consider: Can you guarantee the person you're seeing today who doesn't have an addiction won't develop one in the future?

There are no guarantees in love or life. And that's not what we should be looking for. Like Lainey, on Date Seven, when you're getting ice cream after a movie, you can use what I call a "transition conversation" to bring up those deeper questions. For instance, if you watch a movie that draws on the theme of a challenging time or mental illness, you can say something like, "Wow, the portrayal of that character's anxiety seemed so authentic and vulnerable. Have you ever struggled with anxiety or other mental health struggles?" This creates an opportunity to learn more about your date and potentially also to share about yourself. What you should be looking for in this conversation is clarity and authenticity. And most importantly, you should feel confident that their responses represent a person who is willing to work on themselves—and to work with you—to create the life and relationship you're both longing for.

The Ex Files

You may have shuddered when I mentioned that you need to get clarity on the other person's past relationships. *Cringe.* What you don't know can't hurt you, right?

Wrong.

Although you don't need to go full CSI by stalking their Facebook account back to 2002—investigating everything down to the name of their ex's dog—you should have a basic understanding of what occurred in their past relationships. This should be a snapshot of what went wrong. But more than that, you need to experience how your date processes and talks about these past relationships—how they impacted their life and how that will influence any relationship they have moving forward.

You may be wondering, "Why is the past important? Why can't we just move forward?" The way someone processes past relationships tells us a lot about them. Although you'll want to know some aspects of *what* happened in past relationships, the most important thing is *how* they've processed their past relationships and how they've integrated that learning for future relationships. What meaning do they give to relationships in general now? These are the important questions to ask *before* you become emotionally invested. You don't want to discover that they're in an unhealthy pattern of relationships . . . and you're the next in line.

Before you bring your notebook to the next date to make it feel like an exclusive tell-all interview with Barbara Walters, I want you to know there's a way to ask about this topic that is respectful while still bringing the clarity and information you need. This should happen on a "context and conversation" date: maybe during a paint night or while walking through an art gallery or street festival when you're having fun enjoying the environment and your date is relaxed so they don't feel pressured or defensive.

The first way is to go back to a previous conversation. For instance, maybe your date shared that they've been engaged before. By bringing up information they've already shared with you, you don't have to feel like you're probing or digging, but rather you're continuing and deepening a conversation. You can say something like, "I was thinking about that thoughtful conversation we were having a few dates ago about your past engagement, and I'm wondering if you'd be open to me asking more about it," or "I remember you saying she wasn't the type of person you were looking for in a long-term commitment. Can you share more about why you thought that?"

Approaching the conversation this way, with sensitivity and respect, helps someone feel safe as they share vulnerably with you while still allowing you to hold them to a standard of truth, honesty, and integrity.

Hopefully, they'll be able to give you a clear answer— one that helps you feel comfortable moving forward in your relationship. But what if they say something like, "I'm not sure what she did that made me feel like I didn't want to commit"? Don't just let them off the hook. Ask follow-up questions like, "Has this happened in other past relationships, or did it happen only this once?" or "What would you need to know or feel in order to feel like you *do* want to commit to someone?"

If it's happened with only one person, that's a good sign it was simply a case of incompatibility. If, however, they've felt the same lack of desire to commit to every person they've been in a relationship with, that may be an unhealthy pattern.

Additionally, you want to get clarity about what that person or relationship was missing that made that person not "the one." For example, maybe they didn't share the same values or vision for the future. Maybe one person wanted children and the other didn't. Maybe they had different religious beliefs that they didn't think would be a problem initially but which ended up causing conflict that was only going to increase. The key in conversations about past relationships is to focus on two Ps:

- *Patterns*: Has this happened before?
- *Process*: How have they processed their past, and how does that affect their current beliefs about relationships and the way the past impacts their life and well-being today?

All in the Family

Have you ever heard the saying "When you marry a person, you marry the family"?

Blogger Amanda Magee once wrote that marrying into a family is a lot like traveling the world. When you travel, you adapt to the customs and traditions of the place you're visiting. You learn to be flexible and savor the good moments while assuming things will not always go according to plan.[7]

We know from the field of attachment research that the single most important factor that influences someone's development and the quality of their relationships is their family of origin. How important are family relationships when it comes to the long-term quality of a romantic relationship? Research has found that uncomfortable relationships with in-laws are stressful for spouses, particularly for wives. And the quality of someone's relationship with the in-laws early on predicts how stable, satisfied, and committed the marriage will be.[8]

Although I'd venture to say there are cultural variations in the importance of family relationships and how they impact marriage, the research is clear: They do impact marriage, both in the short term and in the long term, and it's important to be aware of the family dynamics before committing to someone.

One caveat here: While many people are aware of their family's dysfunctional patterns or issues, some people may *not* be aware, because their family of origin is the only family they've experienced.

I've worked with thousands of people over my career who truly didn't understand how their family's emotional health (or lack thereof) impacted them. Many assumed that all families function the way their family functioned. Even if they saw glimpses of other families, no one looking in from the outside truly knows what happens behind closed doors.

Every family has its "stuff." The key is learning how your potential partner interprets their family's "stuff." How do they interpret their family's dynamics in the context of what they observe in the world? How do they speak about their parents? What is their relationship like with their father and mother? Did they come from a two-parent household and, if not, who was their primary caregiver or who did they attach to? What did their family dynamic look like? What were their sibling relationships like? Is their family close-knit, or are they distant from each other? Is there any family history of physical or mental health issues?

All of these questions—and more—are important to help you gain awareness about the dynamic within the family you may be entering, as well as how this person has individuated on their own. A major component is understanding what their parents' relationship dynamic was like as they were growing up and what it's like now. What does the person you're dating hope to re-create and model in their own relationship, and what do they *not* want to emulate in their relationship?

A Note about Cultural Differences

In the field of psychology, literature and many studies have been written from a Western perspective, which means they lack consideration for different cultural backgrounds and belief systems. As a result, we can hyperfocus on ideas such as boundaries, independence, and disconnection without considering that some cultural norms don't fit within a Western definition of "normal" and can be considered "dysfunctional" even if they work well within that particular culture's belief system and organization. For example, a family that's highly involved and connected may be normal for one culture, but for another it may feel too enmeshed and unhealthy.

On the flip side, some family or cultural traditions that are considered the "norm" negatively affect the individual who doesn't want to live that way. If you've seen the movie *My Big Fat Greek Wedding*, you may recall how the main character, Toula, responds to the cultural expectation for women to get married and have a family. She says, "'You'd better get married soon. You're starting to look old.' My dad's been saying that to me since I was fifteen. Because nice Greek girls are supposed to do three things in life: marry Greek boys, make Greek babies, and feed everyone . . . When I was growing up, I knew I was different."[9]

What may have worked well for other women with the same cultural background was not working for Toula individually.

It's ultimately up to you to evaluate which aspects of your cultural background work for you and which aspects have created damage in your life and relationships and are cycles you want to break before having your own committed relationship, marriage, and family.

Anytime you're tempted to label or pathologize your own culture or family of origin, ask yourself these questions:

- How has this value or tradition impacted my life positively?
- How has it impacted me negatively?
- How can I honor my family and culture despite disagreeing with this norm, tradition, or value?
- What is one way I want to do things differently?

Tools

Vision and Values

Date Seven is the time to ask what this person's vision for the future is. You can bring this up directly by saying something like, "You seem like a driven person. What would you want your life to look like in a few years? What would your life look like if all your dreams came true?" Where do they see themselves one year from now, three years from now, five years from now? Knowing someone's vision for their life is crucial when you're considering entering a long-term relationship with them. Many people assume their timelines will magically "intertwine" if they think they're meant to be with each other.

The reality is, your timeline may intersect with someone else's, but you might not be connected on overall timing. Or you might have only a couple of points of connection: *I want to buy a house in the next couple of years too! I'd love to have kids in the next four or five years too! I'd love to travel the world for a few years before having children as well.* When you don't have a clear understanding of someone's broader vision for their life, there's a risk of resentment developing. Why? Because even if your timelines have a point of connection, if either one of you has to make too many adaptations to accommodate the other's vision, resentment will result. Over time, resentment multiplies, which can wreak havoc in a relationship. The most ideal relationship is one where you're going in the same direction with someone you can enjoy the ride with.

Often people find themselves in relationships where they never had discussions about the direction of the relationship. Proverbs 29:18 says, "Where there is no vision, the people perish" (KJV). I believe that without vision, relationships perish as well.

Many people in a relationship wake up one day and don't recognize the person they entered a committed relationship with. A relationship without a unified vision is like a ship trying to go in two different directions. At best, it stays stuck—or moves a few waves forward and many waves back. At worst, it breaks apart and sinks like the *Titanic*, with no room on the raft for Jack to survive. (By the way, I totally think they both could have survived and the movie still would have been a hit. People love a happy ending, right?)

By Date Five hopefully you had a vague idea of the outline of this person's vision, but on Date Seven you need to color in the lines. You need to feel confident that your visions align in the most important ways. While every relationship requires certain compromises, you shouldn't have to make severe sacrifices to stay with this person.

At this point, you may be thinking, "What if someone has a vision but it doesn't come to fruition?" You're not wrong to think this! After all, you don't want to marry someone who's a dreamer and not a doer, who has big visions and fantasies but never makes things happen. Some things are out of our control, and sometimes we're dreaming too small when God has a vision in store for us that is much bigger than we can even imagine. Nonetheless, someone's vision for their life is still important, even if not every part of it becomes reality, because it identifies their values.

Tell me your dreams, and I'll tell you who you are.

When your core values and vision for the future align with the values and vision of the person you're dating, the chances are good you align with this person.

Coaching Corner

The date: A contextuation date where you have extended time focusing on an activity as well as plenty of time for longer conversation.

Ideal amount of time: Up to half a day

Ideal settings: Hike and picnic, horseback riding, music-in-the-park night (with breaks in between), dinner and a movie, local fair or festival, apple-picking.

Dos: Be open and curious. Ask whatever questions you need to seek clarity and make decisions after the date instead of making snap judgments during the date or when you hear new and vulnerable information.

Don'ts: Don't push your vision for the future or your values on your date or question theirs. Don't be judgmental. Date Seven is about listening, not convincing.

Questions to Ask on Date Seven

- Tell me about a previous significant relationship you've had.
- What did you learn about love from your parents' relationship?
- Is there anything you wish were different about your childhood?
- What's your view on mental illness, and are you open to seeking support if you ever struggle?
- What does money mean to you?
- Where do you see yourself next year? In two years? In five years?

Post-Date Seven Reflections

- What did I learn on this date that I didn't know before?
- How do I feel about any previous relationship they had? Is anything they shared a deal-breaker?
- How do we align on family dynamics, views on money, and lifestyle choices?
- Do this person's values and vision align with mine?

You're setting the stage for commitment, and you're almost where you desire to be: in a loving, healthy, and committed relationship! By asking these questions on Date Seven, you're building security and intimacy and gaining clarity so that when you do cross that finish line, you can move forward without fear and feel the way you've always wanted to in a relationship!

DATE EIGHT

The House That Built Him

I have an amazing family and parents I look up to. So why am I constantly attracting these people who seem to be so unhealthy and bad for me?" This was the question my client Hannah asked when we started working together. When I asked her about her parents' relationship, she said, "They set *such* a high standard for me."

After we dug a bit deeper, I told her it was beautiful and wonderful that her parents set such a great example for her *and* that no one is perfect. I pointed out that her parents certainly had some patterns or dynamics that weren't ideal— ones she might not want to emulate in a future relationship. It was important to look at the dynamics of her family and those of Mason's, the guy she was about to go on Date Eight with.

"In the cave we fear to enter lies the treasure that we seek."[1] This quote, often attributed to American author Joseph Campbell, accurately portrays the frightening but rewarding journey we embark on when we seek to discover more about how our past relationships impact the relationship we are trying to create.

In working with singles, I've seen that the main aspect of their inner lives that often creates patterns of self-sabotage is the way they've internalized their relationship with one or both of their parents (or primary caregivers). Lack of awareness about this creates blind spots and roadblocks in their adult relationships. We stay unaware of these dynamics often out of self-protection. It may be too painful to dig into the past. Or if we looked the truth about our parents square in the face, we might not be able to have the relationship with them that we currently have as adults.

Often the challenging parts of our past—such as our parents' relationship—are the very things we must explore to help us understand why we love the way we do, why we have the relationship expectations we do, and why we have the fears about love that we do. It may feel frightening to go there, because it feels like a dark cave with a lot of secrets you may not want to uncover. But it may also contain treasure that will help you finally have the relationship you desire.

Can you live in the gray areas and leave behind the black-and-white, all-or-nothing thinking of the past? Can you admire your parents' relationship and still see where there were gaps or weaknesses? Can you feel deeply loved by your parents yet realize you had certain needs that weren't met? We can live in this tension when we drop our judgment and simply get curious about the relationships and attachments that formed us.

Complete this sentence: "To experience love in my family, I have to . . ."

Gulp. I know. It's a big one.

When we wonder why we don't feel worthy of the great

love we desire, it's often because we don't realize that some-where in our past we internalized that we had to *do* something or *be* a certain way for our parents to truly love us.

Around Date Eight, you may feel a familiar desire: want-ing to prove you're worthy of love and a long-term commit-ment. You may be sucked into the familiar feeling of wanting to earn the love you so deeply desire.

Maybe you're like Hannah. She was a sensitive child who felt loved or unloved by her parents based on how they reacted to her. On some level, she knew they loved her, but it didn't always feel like it. When she misbehaved and they were angry with her, she felt unlovable. Hannah internalized the message that to be loved, she had to be obedient. This translated into people-pleasing and codependent patterns in her romantic relationships.

Just as we may believe we have to earn our parents' love, we often believe the same about God. We don't understand the concept of unconditional love because we always create conditions. "If I'm obedient enough, then I won't be pun-ished." "If I do good things, God will give me what I ask for." It's a performance merry-go-round we can't seem to escape from, whether it's in our relationship with God, our parents, or our future spouse.

As humans, we love conditions because they give us an illusion of control. If we can do enough things that are love-worthy, then they can't ever leave us, right? If we can't earn someone's love, how can we ensure that we will have it forever?

In the movie *Bruce Almighty*, there is a poignant moment when Bruce, the character who took over God's job because he thought he could do it better, tries to make his girlfriend fall back in love with him. He asks God, "How can you make someone love you without affecting free will?" To which God, played by Morgan Freeman, responds, "If you can come up with an answer to that one, let me know!"[2]

We can't control love. We can't make someone love us. What you can control is being the fully authentic version of yourself, unhindered by false assumptions based on misinterpretations of the past. Once we recognize that we've internalized, often subconsciously, these misunderstandings from our parents, we can forgive ourselves, heal the parts of us that feel we must earn love, and work toward loving ourselves, and others, unconditionally.

 **Soul Work**

Understanding Parental Relationship Patterns

Whether you came from a traditional family or not, whether your parents were together or not, their relationship shapes the core story of who you are and what you believe loving someone truly means.

Most of the time, singles I work with tend to categorize their parents' relationships in black-and-white terms. I usually hear things like, "My parents have a great marriage!" or "My parents had the worst marriage ever! I want my relationship to look the opposite."

If this sounds familiar, I encourage you to shift from

viewing your parents' marriage in such a binary way and instead to recognize the nuance and then color in the lines so you can see the gray areas. When we're stuck in black-and-white thinking, we tend to overlook things that could sabotage the future relationship we desire. When people say their parents had a great marriage, they often overlook some ways their parents struggled. And overlooking those areas of struggle may cause them to enter a relationship that exaggerates those struggles but in a different way.

Hannah assumed that her parents' relationship was perfect because she overlooked the slight imperfections that naturally affected their relationship. Because they weren't glaring issues, they were easy to overlook. When I asked her to look a little deeper, she said, "Well, my mom often criticized my dad. She kind of wears the pants in the family, but I think I'd rather be in a more equal relationship with a man I respect and admire. I also know that my parents have different views about politics and faith, which I think created some challenges. They did—and still do—everything together, and I feel like their emotional well-being would often bleed over into the kids and each other. If one person was upset, the other person became upset. It was almost as if we didn't get to have our own feelings. We were very close, but sometimes I wish we'd had the opportunity to have our own opinions without someone being offended if we disagreed with them."

Although Hannah's family was close and loving, they were prone to what psychologists call an "enmeshed" family system, where familial closeness can feel overbearing.[3] In this type of family, parents often receive much of their emotional support from their children. While Hannah's family valued closeness and enjoyed a deep connectedness, it often came with a cost: loss of autonomy and the freedom to be oneself.

Hannah quickly became attached to the guys she dated. She felt deeply connected to them after just a couple of dates. Because of her upbringing, she didn't allow herself the independence and space she needed to see these partners clearly for who they were before she became attached. She assumed all people were like her parents and treated them as such, without letting them show her who they genuinely were. Hannah didn't realize that she was bringing into dating relationships the codependent dynamic that was so familiar to her, hindering her from creating the relationship she truly desired.

After we worked together, Hannah was able to see her parents for who they were—good people in a good marriage who still had real flaws. She could view their weaknesses without guilt or disrespect but rather with awareness as she asked herself some important questions: "What qualities did my parents display in their relationship that I'd want in a future relationship of my own? What qualities did my parents display that I don't want to replicate in a future relationship? How did their marriage influence my beliefs about love?"

The Parent Pendulum

For my client Andrea, the opposite was true. Her parents were immigrants from a country in which marriages were determined by family input and obligation to the community. In Andrea's evaluation, her parents didn't have a good marriage. They had married because of duty and family relations, but they had no chemistry or "spark." She viewed her parents' marriage as "all bad," and she wanted the opposite.

Andrea was experiencing what I call the parent pendulum effect. It's when you grow up with a dynamic you don't like—one that affects you in some way—and then later, in your own relationship, you swing the pendulum to the opposite extreme in an effort not to replicate that dynamic. Ideally, though, you should land with the pendulum somewhere in the middle—aware of your generational upbringing and intentional in the choices you're making for yourself rather than being reactive to that upbringing and going too far in the other direction.

What Andrea didn't realize was that there were aspects of her parents' relationship she *did* want to emulate. When I asked her, "What do you admire about your parents' relationship?" it took her a second, but she told me she admired their commitment and loyalty despite the adversity they faced. She admired their shared values and similar personality traits. They had stayed married even in the face of difficult times. When pressed, Andrea was able to look deeper and see the good gray—the blend of black and white that makes for the whole story.

As we evaluated Andrea's dating history, we realized it was affected by her habit of swinging the pendulum to the other extreme. She was stuck in a cycle of never getting past a month of dating someone. She tended to meet potential partners at casual locations, such as the gym or a bar, and she often had witty conversations with guys she connected with on dating apps. Often they bonded over shared activities.

But there was no depth, no duty, no talk of commitment. On Date Eight, I encouraged Andrea to reflect on her dynamic with Will, the guy she had been dating, and notice what aspects seemed to mirror the positive qualities of her parents' relationship.

I told her that while she might not want a duplicate of her parents' relationship, what she was looking for probably wasn't on the opposite side of the spectrum; rather, it was most likely somewhere in the middle. I told her that Date Eight was the right place for her to clarify whether Will embodied the values of devotion and commitment that were qualities she admired about her parents' relationship.

Andrea made a mistake many of us make when we see our parents' relationship as all bad: she allowed the pendulum to swing too far in the other direction because she wanted to get as far away from their dynamic as possible. That often lands us at the other extreme, which is, let's face it, still extreme. Because she saw her parents' relationship in a negative light, she assumed all she needed in a relationship was chemistry—the thing her parents didn't have. But what she didn't understand was that a relationship that is all chemistry and no commitment is destined for failure. She needed to ask more directly, on Date Eight, about Will's views on commitment and marriage and also explore the model his parents had demonstrated for him to ensure that they weren't connecting only on the basis of chemistry.

We're looking to create our perfect love story, so we start overvaluing and overemphasizing what our parents' story lacked instead of considering that it's just one piece of the larger puzzle. As we talked about in Date Six, we're more likely to view things through the lens of negativity bias and see what we, as well as our family members, lack, rather than viewing things from a positive perspective and recognizing what they *did* have that worked.

When we let our subconscious drive the bus, we often look for a love story that's all about finding the missing piece of our parents' love story. Or we look to mimic their dynamic (for better or for worse). Both searches leave us unsatisfied when we are unaware of how our understanding of our parents' relationship affects who we choose for a partner.

Dissecting the "Daddy Issues"

By Date Eight, you may have uncovered a lot of information about yourself and about the person you're dating. But there's an area we haven't yet covered that we *have* to dive into, because I can't write a dating book without demystifying one of the biggest and best-known myths out there.

You've probably heard about the concept of "daddy issues," where a girl dates emotionally unavailable men because she had an emotionally unavailable dad. She's trying to resolve these issues by dating the same kind of guy over and over again, hoping one of them will show her the love she's always desired from her father.

While this concept isn't entirely off base, it's often a bit more nuanced than we think.

It's frequently assumed that when people struggle to attract healthy partners, it's because the dynamic with their partner mirrors the relationship they had with the parent of the opposite sex. As I mentioned earlier, it's more accurate to say that it's because of the way our parents' relationship impacted our beliefs about the meaning of love, marriage, and relationships.

In my experience, we tend to relate to and embody more characteristics of one parent and idealize or want to be like the other parent. *This* is the dynamic that is playing out when we're looking to form a relationship with someone.

That was the case for Charlotte. A successful executive, Charlotte couldn't figure out what was going wrong in her dating life. "I have the best relationship with my dad. We're best friends, and he taught me everything I know in my career. We spent my whole childhood traveling, being outdoors. My parents had a great relationship. And yet I constantly attract these bad-boy guys who make me feel like I'm not worthy, despite all my success. What's going on?"

While Charlotte believed that her parents had a great relationship, something significant emerged when we dug a bit deeper. Yes, her connection with her dad was strong. But her relationship with her mom? It had some challenges.

"My mom and I have a good relationship, but I always felt like she was the harsher critic and that I had to earn her approval and love," she confessed. "I guess we didn't really understand each other, but I desperately wanted to feel understood by her and to feel worthy."

Bingo.

While Charlotte was most aligned with her dad's personality and values, she kept attracting men who made her feel like her mom often made her feel.

Charlotte's dating challenges weren't a result of daddy issues. Rather, she still had the internal soundtrack of her mom's criticism playing in her head, which made her feel like she wasn't good enough. She was chasing approval and love from guys who reminded her of her mom. And that "chase" felt familiar and attractive to her because it echoed the dynamic she experienced as a kid.

Now, I'm not going to blame everything (or really anything) on Charlotte's parents. Charlotte's parents were nurturing, loving, and supportive. They had a good, healthy relationship, *and* they were human. They had weaknesses and flaws. And you shouldn't blame your parents either. Parents do the best they can with the tools they have at the time. Does that excuse unacceptable or abusive behavior? Absolutely not. But the goal of dissecting family dynamics isn't to play the blame game. If you've learned anything from this book, I hope it's the concept of taking personal responsibility and focusing only on what you can control, leaving the rest to God and the right timing, trusting that everything will work out for good if you're doing the work only *you* can do.

Charlotte—and all of us—need to realize that sometimes we attract the extreme version of our parents' negative traits. Charlotte's mom may have been mildly critical of her, but because of her negative bias, Charlotte amplified that criticism to attract someone who made her feel woefully unworthy. This is an extreme version of the mild criticism she received as a child, because as children, everything is amplified for us. We can also tend to attract the negative versions of our parents' healthy selves. Maybe her mom just gave her a *feeling* of unworthiness, but it lingered with Charlotte to the point that she started attracting people who were a version of her mom in order to write a happy ending to the unresolved story from her childhood.

Charlotte fell into the trap we all do when we have "daddy issues"—or rather, issues attracting emotionally or otherwise unavailable people. "If this person chose me," we think, "it must mean something about me. It must mean I'm finally worthy." But we don't have to fall into that trap. We can honor our childhood desires and fantasies while simultaneously offering forgiveness and compassion to that younger version of ourselves who innocently misunderstood her experiences and internalized her need for love in the wrong way.

We look for the unavailable parent in a potential partner, ready to write ourselves a happy ending, but we've cast the same character in the same role—the person we want to love us unconditionally. We look for the same character traits that made for a sad childhood story and then wonder why we're stuck.

 **Strategy**

Beware of the EIBA Mistake

On Date Eight, you're going to dive deeper into some of the areas we outlined in Date Seven, because you're assessing whether you're going to take the leap of faith into a committed relationship with this person.

I've done a lot of work counseling couples in premarital therapy. It's always quite shocking how many of these couples, bright-eyed and full of optimism, became *engaged* before they understood important details about each other and the other issues we're covering in Dates Seven through Ten. I can't help but imagine that a huge reason many married people report low levels of satisfaction is because they made what I call the EIBA mistake:

Emotionally
Invested
Before
Aware

This is why I recommend you ask these questions *now*, before you define the relationship—and certainly before you get engaged or married. Many people tell me they wish they'd asked these questions before they married their ex.

If you take away one thing from this book, let it be this: Remember to become aware *before* you invest emotionally. If you need to write the letters *EIBA* on your hand with a permanent marker and look at it while you're out on a date, by all means, go for it!

Okay, now for the questions. These will help you get to the root of your own parents' relationship dynamics and the ones present in your potential partner's family.

First, you'll want to talk about communication styles. Here are a few questions to get you started: How did your family communicate while you were growing up? How do they communicate now? Is their style direct and factual, or is it more affectionate and lighthearted? Did you feel you were able to freely communicate your emotions (both negative and positive)?

Next, you'll want to discuss conflict resolution. As you talk, here are some topics to bring up: Would you describe conflict resolution in your family as calm, constructive, or collaborative? What was the volume level? Was shouting or loud speaking normal, or was it rare and usually a sign of anger? Did anyone in your family experience abuse—physical, mental, emotional—as a part of conflict resolution? Was there stonewalling, such as giving someone the "silent treatment" or refusing to cooperate or communicate?

Then you'll want to talk about how their family showed love and care for one another. How did your family display and communicate love? What were the primary love languages (for example, quality time, acts of service, words of affirmation, physical touch)?[4] How did they repair conflict: Was it fully forgiven in love, or were grudges common and past hurts brought up?

Finally, you can delve into their parents' marriage and relationship. What was their primary motivation for being married—Love? Tradition? Shared culture? Convenience? Was it a default next step? If they stayed married, what seemed to hold the marriage together during difficult times? Did they value connection and the sharing of life together, or did they seem to prefer living independent lives?

Answering these and other strategic questions is important for understanding yourself as well as your potential partner. Their level of awareness or the degree to which they've thought through these dynamics or processed them on their own is also important to consider. If someone hasn't done that, they may not realize how their family impacts them. They're also probably not aware that they have the choice to either repeat or break the cycles and patterns they saw in their parents' relationship.

You may be wondering, "How do I bring up these direct questions during the Date Eight conversation?" The answer: Having a family-focused date can be a fun way to get to know each other. Maybe you meet a sibling or cousin or spend time in your date's hometown, à la *The Bachelor*'s hometown dates. You don't necessarily have to meet the parents yet, especially if your date is not very close with their parents or doesn't introduce many people to them.

While they're showing you around their hometown, like walking by the field where they played baseball, you can bring up questions like, "Was your dad the type to coach you from the stands, or was he a silent supporter?" Learning about "the house that built" him, as Miranda Lambert would sing it, will tell you what you need to know before building a future with him.

Tools

Parent Alignment Test

How can you prevent the parent pendulum effect from sabotaging your love life? One way to start is by using a tool I call the parent alignment test. Date Eight is the ideal time to understand your parents' dynamic and understand which role you align with most—and which role your date aligns with most. This involves reflecting on the following questions: How is he similar to the parent I most align with? How is he similar to the parent I most wanted approval from?

How am I similar to the parent he most aligns with? How am I similar to the parent he wanted approval from?

Getting the answers to these questions helps you become aware of the unhealthy patterns you could potentially fall into. When you're aware of something, that's when you can truly work to change it.

The Wait to Feel Worthy

If you're approaching Date Eight and you realize you're still stuck in trying to prove your worth, it's time to take a peek at your list of things that you're looking for in someone. Review that list, and review how this person you're dating makes you feel. Is their character consistent? Is their communication clear and intentional? Are they moving forward and progressing in the relationship?

It's crucial to stop and reflect, because some of us wake up as we're about to go on Date Eight, ready to start calling someone our boyfriend, only to realize we're forming an attachment to the "chase" rather than to the person. We think the soon-to-be relationship is going well, only to find out that the only thing going well is our performance—we're gaining someone's approval.

News flash for all of you would-be pageant queens who want everyone to like you: You haven't been making your thumbs bleed swiping on the dating apps to win a popularity contest. You're looking for a future life partner, not a crown, a sash, and a title.

How do you know if you're bringing this "chasing approval"

dynamic to your dating life? Ask yourself, "Does the person I'm interested in make me feel safe, or is it the attention and approval from them that's making me feel special?"

What's the difference? you may ask.

If someone who doesn't give love away freely—let's say they're a typical "bad boy"—and won't settle down for just anyone has gone on *eight* dates with you, you're probably starting to feel pretty good about yourself. And you may be using this potential relationship to feed your need for desirability—to be liked, loved, and made to feel special.

If he could like *me* when he doesn't like anyone easily . . .

If he can commit to *me* when he never commits to anyone . . .

If he could have any girl but he wants and chooses *me* . . .

We look for this outward stamp of approval when we haven't felt it from our parents, allowed ourselves to receive it from God, or given it to ourselves.

This is also why someone who gives us unconditional, consistent love and approval without us feeling like we've done enough to "prove" our worth may seem unattractive to us. When someone consistent, steady, and intentional is pursuing us and we don't have to prove ourselves worthy to them, we may feel like the relationship came too easily. "Maybe they're desperate for a relationship," we think. "Maybe anyone with a pulse would be fine for them!"

If you're a person of faith, you may have even felt this way about God's love, which is unconditional and for all people. You may have felt like it's not that "special" because everyone can access it.

This is why the story of the prodigal son often ruffles feathers.

If you're unfamiliar with the story, it's found in Luke 15. The way this parable is often recounted, the prodigal son is usually the star of the story. He asks his dad for his part of the inheritance (while the dad is still alive—talk about disrespect!), then runs off and squanders it on booze, babes, and the rest of the bad vices before ending up living with some pigs. Not your typical Hallmark love story, but stick with me. Now he's broke and alone, thinking, "I'd be better off working for my dad as a slave." And so the prodigal son heads back to his home in the ultimate walk of shame, but his dad welcomes him with open arms, throws a huge party, and rejoices that his lost son has been found. Happy ending, right?

Not for the older brother. He's been loyal to his dad, and when he sees all this taking place, instead of rejoicing, he becomes bitter. He's been working steadily every day, proving how great a son he is to his dad, and he basically feels left out and taken for granted. The words of his father strike a deep chord: "'My son,' the father said, 'you are always with me, and everything I have is yours'" (Luke 15:31).

What? The audacity! The brother has been working all this time, looking for approval, wanting to feel special, only to realize he didn't have to work for it at all? All his accolades, accomplishments, and acts of service he did to make his dad proud of him—and his dad would have loved him the same even without them?

Yes, exactly.

The Love You're Looking For

I bet you never heard this analogy in Sunday school, but we're often like the older brother in our dating life. We put our best foot forward, wear our nice perfume, share how well we're doing at work, try to express how well-liked and educated and smart and funny and attractive we are, and we think, "This will make me special and worthy. I'll *finally* get to prove my worthiness. Someone will look at all my accomplishments, my positive characteristics, and my outward appearance and reward me with a relationship."

In truth, the love and approval you're looking for have been there all along.

When you date from a place of *already* feeling worthy, you will likely attract the healthy relationship and love you long for because you're not looking for a stamp of approval. You're simply looking for a love you can relax into and for an opportunity to live out the worthiness you already inherently have. If you enter a relationship to prove your worthiness, you will always have another mountain to climb. You'll pass one arbitrary threshold of worthiness only to face another one down the road.

Trying to prove our worth, like the older brother in the parable of the prodigal son, doesn't lead to a healthy relationship. But trying to establish a relationship when we feel unworthy of love, like the younger brother, doesn't work well either. The passage from Luke says when the prodigal son realized that his father's servants received better treatment than he did on the farm where he was working, he decided to return home—to live in the unconditional love he already had from his father.

> So he got up and went to his father.
> But while he was still a long way off, his father saw him and was filled with compassion for him; he ran to his son, threw his arms around him and kissed him.
> The son said to him, "Father, I have sinned against heaven and against you. *I am no longer worthy* to be called your son." (Luke 15:20–21, emphasis added)

He thought his mistakes qualified him for rejection and deemed him unworthy of receiving love. And that's what many of us believe. We often disqualify ourselves from a healthy relationship because we feel unworthy, either because of what we've done or what we haven't done well enough.

> But the father said to his servants, "Quick! Bring the best robe and put it on him. Put a ring on his finger and sandals on his feet. Bring the fattened calf and kill it. Let's have a feast and celebrate. For this son of mine was dead and is alive again; he was lost and is found." So they began to celebrate. (Luke 15:22–24)

We settle for conditional love all the time, but what we truly seek is transformational love. We don't want to have to prove our worth. We don't want someone to look at us and think of all the ways we can improve, be better, and show that we're good enough. We want them to see us like the father sees the prodigal son.

We want them to love us not for what we do but for who we are.

You'll know your date is the right person when you can relax into your inherent worthiness. And when they see you a long way off, with all your flaws, with all your past mistakes, with all your future fears, they will have compassion on you and love you. They'll breathe a sigh of relief and say, "Ah, there she is. She was lost, and now she's found."

Coaching Corner

The date: Hometown or family vibes

Ideal amount of time: This date can last a full day.

Ideal settings: A day trip somewhere that's family friendly or a fun "hometown" style date, visiting where one of you grew up or doing an activity you enjoyed when you were younger. Bonus points if a long drive is involved, allowing you to dive into deeper questions!

Dos: Imagine them as their younger self, and lead with grace rather than judgment. Respect that no one's parents are perfect; they were likely doing the best they could at the time. It's always best to lead with empathy and goodwill.

Don'ts: Don't shy away from the tough, honest, and vulnerable conversations. Now is the time to have them! And don't force a response out of someone as if you're hosting a true crime podcast. Explore these sensitive topics with grace. If they say something that makes you wonder, "Is this a deal-breaker?," don't react right away; sleep on it. Sometimes the shock of hearing the difficult parts of someone's upbringing and family dynamics can create a "fight or flight" trauma response. Instead, acknowledge how difficult it is to be vulnerable, and take time to process this information before deciding about the potential relationship.

Questions to Ask on Date Eight

- What was the best thing about the family you were raised in?
- What was the hardest thing?
- Tell me about your parents' marriage. What did you think of it as a child? What do you think of it now?
- How does your parents' relationship impact what you're looking for in a relationship?

Post-Date Eight Reflections

- What did I learn from the parent alignment test?
- In what ways has my parents' relationship impacted my expectations of marriage?
- In what ways am I still trying to measure up or feel worthy in this new relationship?

You have to dig deep in Date Eight to experience the true, beyond-the-surface connection and intimacy you long for, and it starts with understanding your core story, being aware of the relationships that have shaped you, and embodying your inherent worthiness.

No Bad Parts

I t seems like the stars are aligning." Natasha was beaming as she told me about Ryan. "Everything seems to be going so well, not in a 'too good to be true' sort of way but in an authentic way."

I was happy for her and recommended that she reflect on past dates and see if there were any behaviors or comments regarding Ryan's emotional or mental health that caused her to pause.

"He did mention once on Date Two that he had dealt with depression on and off, but it hasn't come up since then."

Bingo.

"That's the sort of question you want to ask on Date Nine," I told her. "It's important to start exploring and learning about the more vulnerable things, what some would call the 'shadow side,' that he may not have felt comfortable sharing too much about when he first met you. But now as you're approaching a committed relationship, it's important for you to know."

If you've made it to Date Nine, like Natasha, you may

be thinking, "Well, I'm almost there, right? One more date should solidify that they're my soulmate."

This is the case for many of my clients who've gone through the soul work and strategy presented thus far and feel confident in progressing their relationship to the next level. But for others? Well, it doesn't work out so well for them. They've simply gone through the motions—and then wonder why they haven't figured out by Date Nine if they're dating Mr. Right or Mr. Right Now.

Although I'm a doctor, I'm not an "Is there a doctor on the plane?" kind of doctor. I'm more of an "I can help you breathe through your fear of flying" doctor. However, the best analogy I can think of as you approach Date Nine is that of a properly aligned spine. If you've dealt with any type of back problems, you know that if there's any misalignment in your spine, it's painful—and it's time to adjust. That's how I want you to think about Date Nine: *Are we aligned?*

As I told Natasha, Ryan's struggle with depression was not a red flag or deal-breaker on its own by any means. After all, we all have a shadow side—mental health challenges (or potential for them) or things we will carry into the relationship that are messy. But the truth is, we're not looking for perfection; we're looking for alignment.

We explored in Dates Seven and Eight how our past has impacted our present. We unpacked our family dynamics and our past relationships. And we discussed our values and hopes for the future. We've established that, from a compatibility perspective, the more our pasts are similar, and the more our future vision is similar, the better opportunity we have to create a healthy and happy relationship. We've learned where they've come from and determined that we both know where we want to go and are headed in the same direction. We've established chemistry, compatibility, and connection and can see this person as our life partner. Now in Date Nine we explore how to build a safe and healthy "emotional home" for the relationship we're potentially about to enter.

Building an Emotional Home for the Relationship

When someone struggles with their mental health as Ryan admitted to, this often affects both their internal world and their external world. It shifts how they understand themselves and others. I'd often heard, growing up in Sunday school and reading the four gospels, that the four writers of the books, Matthew, Mark, Luke, and John, documented eyewitness accounts of the same events, but they did so from different perspectives because of their own vantage point, their own life experiences, and their own lens. For example, Luke was a doctor by profession, so he tended to go into detail about Jesus's healing of physical illnesses. John, on the other hand, seemed to have a more poetic approach and was more of a storyteller. Matthew was an accountant and tax collector, and in his gospel he found it important to give a detailed account of the genealogy of Jesus (such a CPA move to get a detailed history would be a dreaded chore for anyone else).

An individual's struggle with mental health within the

context of a relationship can be likened to two individuals experiencing the same events but understanding them from their own unique perspectives. One person with a particular mental health struggle may see relational conflict through their specific lens and create different meaning than someone who doesn't have that struggle. For Natasha, it was important to learn more about Ryan's struggles with depression to understand how it could impact him individually in the future as well as how it would certainly impact their potential shared life.

We have to remember that mental health struggles exist on a spectrum and aren't black and white. Each person experiences their struggle differently, and support and help are available for most mental health challenges. What I emphasized to Natasha was that she should focus on Ryan the person, not on his "problem." In a society obsessed with labels and categorizing, this can be hard to do.

On Date Nine, I recommended that Natasha and Ryan go to a used bookstore since reading classic novels was a shared hobby of theirs. They took my advice. While at the bookstore, they perused different books and had conversations about their favorite authors. Natasha came across a vintage copy of *War and Peace*, the one-thousand-page novel by Leo Tolstoy, and commented about his ability to write such a masterpiece even though he struggled with his mental health and depression. Ryan vulnerably shared that often his own writing of poetry and short stories had helped him get through some difficult bouts of depression. It was the opening Natasha needed to ask Ryan the questions she had to have answered to feel comfortable moving forward.

Strategy

Assessing Alignment

On Date Nine, I want you to spend time reflecting on whether you've thoroughly understood the alignment of your connection with the person you're dating, noting the potential speed bumps that every relationship is bound to face in its own way.

One area I want to highlight on Date Nine that is crucial for the process of "snapping back" into alignment is understanding someone's emotional context. As we discussed in Date Three, it's important to see someone "in context," because that's the way you will truly understand their character. And a huge aspect of emotional context involves your date's current and past mental health and their inner emotional world.

While I believe our current society is prone to diagnosing everyone with some sort of disorder and thinking everyone and their mom is a "narcissist" (hint: some people are just jerks), I do think it's important to be aware of your own and your potential partner's mental health history and the way they preemptively take care of themselves and stay in "prevention mode"—working on themselves before there are any actual problems.

In my experience, we all have the potential to struggle with mental health. No one is immune. However, if we know how to take care of ourselves when "triggers" threaten to activate our negative predispositions and we're open and willing to get help, we will be equipped to handle any issues that arise.

So how does mental health relate to dating? As a therapist and dating coach, I regularly see people navigating mental health struggles in their relationships or trying to make sense of what went wrong in the past with potential relationships. I've come to understand that relationships often don't make it because of unexamined mental health struggles. Potentially great relationships either never have the chance to grow or are doomed before they even begin because of mental health challenges that haven't been worked through.

As we navigate these complex topics together, I ask that you keep a few things in mind.

The first is the premise I began this book with: Every person is worthy and deserving of love. There is truly a lid for every pot. Every relationship has a unique set of challenges and a unique set of gifts. Struggling with mental health does not disqualify you in any way from finding the right person. By the same token, just because someone struggles with their mental health does not mean you should stop exploring a relationship with them.

 **Tools**

Mental Health Inventory

Although you, or your date, may not have a mental health condition, Date Nine is the place to take inventory of your date's general mental health, the areas where they struggle, and the ways they take care of these areas of their life so they won't struggle in the future. As with other types of health, such as physical health, no one is perfect; we all have areas we can improve in. Date Nine is the place you want to dig a little deeper to understand their mental and emotional world, both their strengths and their areas of struggle.

We all have our own struggles, but sometimes in relationships we cater to the other person if they're going through what we perceive as more "legitimate" challenges. The problem is that resentment can build up so you feel like there isn't room for you to struggle as well. This dynamic can create lasting harm in a relationship, and it's often the partner who isn't struggling, or isn't struggling in that moment, who ends up floundering and breaking off the relationship because they haven't been taking care of their own needs, which causes them to communicate in passive-aggressive and harmful ways.

Second, you need to have a plan of action, or a "prevention plan," in place and learn about what that is for this person. Even if they've never struggled with their mental or emotional health in the past, they should be building what I call a "resilience record": doing the work to stay healthy, which will help them weather the storms when difficulties arise.

It's a common Western belief that there's only one way to work through mental health struggles, and while some mental illnesses are more successfully addressed with treatments such as talk therapy and medication, different cultures find support in different ways. There isn't a one-size-fits-all solution, but your potential partner should be aware of what triggers them, what behaviors and responses don't work well for them and could harm other people (and your relationship), what they can do preventively, and what they would do in an aftercare situation if they did act in unhealthy ways. The key here is that they need to be already working on this or have some level of awareness. This should *not* be an effort led by you.

After learning more about Ryan's struggle with depression, Natasha felt positive hearing about his comprehensive plan that he'd already been applying for several years, including therapy, a support group at church, and exercise. She felt relieved she wouldn't be trying to convince him to seek help when he had a depressive episode, but rather would be beside him as he sailed his own ship through emotionally stormy weather.

Even if someone you're dating isn't currently struggling with a diagnosable mental health condition, it's still important that they (and you yourself!) have a preventive wellness plan. Just because someone isn't struggling with mental health right now doesn't mean they never will.

I often tell my clients it's better to date someone who's struggling right now but is getting help or is willing to get help in the future, than someone who appears to have it all together but thinks they're above seeking help if a difficult situation were to arise. Such a person is naive to all the plot twists life can throw at them, and they lack the humility to embrace their humanity and be open to growing, learning, and adapting along the way. They probably also wouldn't have a reserve of empathy and support should *you* ever struggle with your mental health, and they wouldn't be able to encourage you in your own quest for wellness and might even shame you for your desire to seek help.

Be with someone who is open, honest, and humble about their struggles and isn't above saying, "I need help." This will serve you, your relationship, and your future family in the years to come.

Some great questions to ask on Date Nine are, "If we were ever to face challenges as a couple, would you be open to receiving couples therapy? What other type of support would you be open to if we decide to move forward?"

If they already have good systems and self-care practices in place, that's a major positive. To go with a home renovations analogy, it's like having a desire to build a Spanish-style house. But before you start building, you find an existing house that already has the columns and tiles in the same style you want. Instead of having to start from scratch, you've found a match that aligns with exactly what you're looking for. In the same way, if someone has already been working on themselves in an intentional way, then you have a head start in building a happy and healthy life together.

A Note about Mental Health Support

In Western culture, therapy and medication have been the recommended course of treatment for many mental health struggles. The truth is, traditional talk therapy has existed only since the late 1800s, but people have been getting married and coming together in relationships since Adam and Eve were blaming each other in the garden. (I would have recommended couples therapy right about the time they started scapegoating each other with, "He wasn't there to stop me!" and "She made me do it!")

Different cultures utilize many beneficial types of care that support mental health, including church and community support, support groups, somatic practices such as mindful breathing, community healing practices, acupuncture, herbal medicine, and the list goes on.

The point isn't always what type of help and support your date is receiving or open to; it's understanding if they are intentionally taking care of their physical, emotional, mental, and spiritual health. Additionally, an important question to ask is, Is what they're doing creating self-awareness, harmony, and balance for living a fulfilled and fruitful life? If it's not, are they able to pivot and keep trying new things until they find a regimen that works?

People often get stuck in their mental health journey because they view it as a one-and-done deal. They think, "I went to therapy once, but it didn't work," or "I started taking supplements for natural healing for my depression, but they weren't making a difference."

What gave Natasha peace was Ryan's acceptance that he wasn't immune to depression rearing its ugly head again. If it came, it would not catch him by surprise.

It's important to realize that our mental health is challenged each and every day. Every day, withdrawals are taken out of our mental health bank that can impair our relationships and quality of life. The good news is, we can make deposits to replace those withdrawals if we want to support the life we're trying to create.

Natasha was often the go-to fix-it person in her friend

group. For her own relationship, she needed someone who could support her reciprocally. She had so much to give but desired to start pouring from an overflowing cup instead of an empty one, which was her norm. If you tend to be the giver and the caretaker in your friend group, or if you were the "good kid" who never made any waves in your family, and now you're the person people tend to rely on, your dependability may help you maintain good relationships with friends and family, but it may also mean you naturally attract people prone to needing help that they're not getting on their own. This is because you've gotten your worth and validation from constant giving without a lot of receiving. You may have even internalized that the only way to receive love is to give to and help others continually, to the detriment of your own wants and needs.

While talking about mental health is tough, asking the tough questions *before* entering a committed relationship saves a lot of time and protects us from heartache and emotional damage. Sometimes we ask the important questions too late, after we're already invested in someone. At this point, we usually don't want to give up on our investment in them because we'd be saying goodbye to that person, sure; but we'd also be saying goodbye to the part of ourselves we gave to that person. We would also be saying goodbye to the dream of what we thought we could be together.

And that, whether we acknowledge it or not, is often the most painful part of all.

We'd have to acknowledge we were wrong.

We'd have to tell our friends and family that another relationship bit the dust.

The shame of *still* being single often keeps us in the

wrong relationships because we hope things will change or we hope we're being too dramatic about the red flags. Our emotions have clouded our judgment, and that's when we start normalizing behaviors and letting the high standards we've set begin to slip. The good news is, if you gain clarity on Date Nine, you no longer have to worry about your blind spots and can move forward with someone who is as committed to growth and wholeness as you are.

Always the Bridesmaid

On Date Nine, it's time to take a good look and objectively evaluate—with a trusted friend or family member, support group, or personal therapist—whether you're fully aware of the factors that could affect your relationship.

As someone who clearly would have fit in the "always a bridesmaid, never a bride" category before I got married, I've been a bridesmaid in twenty-two weddings. Twenty. Two. (I'm trying to beat Katherine Heigl's *27 Dresses* count, since I'm still waiting on a few of my best friends' weddings, and maybe one of my clients will throw me a bone and put me in one of theirs—no pressure, though!) Plus, I've supported many friends, family members, and clients in the process leading up to marriage.

One of my friends who was about to walk down the aisle confided in me and her other bridesmaids that she had hesitations about getting married. None of us were married at the time, so it was hard for us to know if these doubts were normal. Was she just getting cold feet, or were these doubts valid enough to call off the wedding?

Now, looking back, I realize there's a lot you don't know before you get married. But if you're experiencing intense anxiety and noticing patterns of unhealthy behavior in the other person before you walk down the aisle, you need friends, family, and supportive people in your life to tell you it's okay not to move forward. As the saying goes, it's better to admit you walked through the wrong door than to live your life in the wrong room.

You're not required to carry anyone's burden, continue in a relationship, or enter a committed relationship if you're not sure about it. In a healthy relationship, there must be space for your needs. You should have a clear picture of someone's faults and struggles, and you should see a commitment to improvement, to the development of self-awareness, and to growth.

Potential in the Room

"Don't marry potential." I've seen this warning plastered on plenty of internet memes and have repeated it in plenty of group chats, trying to convince one of my girlfriends not to give another afraid-of-commitment, emotionally unavailable man a chance.

But I'll let you in on a little secret: *We all marry potential.*
I know—scandalous, right?

The reality is, we're always assessing situations—and potential partners—based on the information in front of us. Are they compatible? Could they be a good fit for us? We make the best guess with the information we have. And the truth? There is always a part of someone that is yet to be discovered. There are always aspects of someone that we will never know, and they may not even know yet themselves. When you say "I do," the cold hard truth is that you're saying "I do" to three people: the person in front of you, the person they were before you met them, and the person they will become in the future.

One of those people you will never meet—the person they were before you met them—but you will encounter shadows of that person in both the things that trigger them and the things that light them up like a little boy again.

One of those people you will meet in the future, in a thousand little words, in tiny exchanged glances as you're juggling toddlers and coordinating your family calendar and living life together. You will grow together and make memories as you meet each other in new ways every day.

And one of those people is the one you've been getting to know. Most of their patterns you can identify by now, but some you're still learning. Even if you feel like you've known them forever, you will be growing in understanding no matter how long you date them. They may still surprise you as you process who they are in real time.

As renowned relationship therapist and expert Esther Perel once said, "In the West today most people are going to have two or three marriages, two or three committed relationships in their adult life. It's just that some of us are going to do it with the same person."[1]

We can deny this reality, convincing ourselves that we know someone completely. Or we can accept that we can only know someone to a certain extent and that we're always saying yes to the lifelong adventure of learning about them.

Coaching Corner

The date: It could be fun to go back to that little coffee shop where you had your first date. Most importantly, make sure you're in an environment where you can have an in-depth conversation.

Ideal amount of time: Half a day to a full day

Ideal setting: This will be an important conversation date. Choose a place where you can hear each other well while still being in a public setting. A park or beach picnic is a great idea. A museum, art gallery, or bookstore would also work well.

Dos: Keep the focus on your date's growth mindset, how willing they are to work on themselves, and how capable they are of making space for your needs, not just their own.

Don'ts: Just like in Date Eight, this is the time to put some important stuff on the table. Don't hold back, but also don't forget to bring your grace, compassion, and curiosity with you.

Questions to Ask on Date Nine

- Have you or do you ever struggle with your mental health? If so, what was/is that like? How did/do you deal with it?
- Are you committed to seeking health and growth in your life? What about in a marriage?
- Are you committed to premarital and marriage therapy for the health of a relationship?

Post-Date Nine Reflections

- How did it feel to talk about my mental health struggles with this person? Did I feel safe? Did I feel heard?
- How did I feel about this person's openness or resistance to individual and marriage therapy?
- How do I feel about what this person revealed to me? Do I feel like I need to take a bit more time to process this information (a few weeks)? Why or why not?
- Did these conversations demonstrate a commitment to growth and humility, or were they laced with defensiveness and pride?

In case you haven't noticed by now, finding your person isn't simply a matter of checking off a bunch of boxes. It's a matter of understanding yourself, understanding the other person, and being open and flexible about working on building a future together. If you can do this, you're ready for Date Ten!

DATE TEN

Ten out of Ten

I think he's going to ask me to be official," Sara told me. She was overjoyed and feeling more at peace, excited, and sure of herself than she had ever been at the start of a relationship. In the past, she tended to rush the "defining the relationship" conversation before she really knew the person, simply because she wanted the security of having a label. But now she realized that things with Ben were different.

"In some ways," I told her, "you may feel like the dating journey is reaching its conclusion, but in reality, the journey is just beginning!"

If, like Sara, you've not already had *the* conversation, I'm going to walk you through the process of transitioning into a committed relationship from a place of expression—where you can fully be yourself—and peace, rather than expectation and demand.

People often approach what's colloquially known as the "DTR," or "define the relationship," conversation by asking direct questions that make the other person defensive and anxious. It's forceful rather than flowing. The person being asked the "what are we" question often feels like they've done something wrong.

Instead, when you feel the natural transition and want to shift into a committed relationship with someone, expressing your feelings and speaking from your heart are the best ways to ensure that the start of your relationship is a healthy one.

If you've arrived at Date Ten, it means that someone has proven they are a compatible and healthy partner with whom you can build the type of relationship you're looking for.

- They've met the main criteria you're looking for.
- You have chemistry and a good connection with them.
- You've addressed the five critical areas, feeling aware and confident of their vision for the future, their values, their family dynamics, their past relationship history, and their mental health.
- You've learned about their character, which has been consistent over time: in different physical contexts (context dates); in different emotional contexts (for example, stuck in traffic, after a bad day at work, after a disagreement with you); and with different people (you've met their friends and/or family, and they've met yours).
- They've demonstrated consistent communication and intentionality in pursuing you. Your frequency of dates and the amount of time you've spent together have increased (you're not just going on one date a week). Additionally, the date frequency hasn't been all-or-nothing or sporadic (for example, they're not blowing up your phone and hanging out with you every day for two weeks, then disappearing for two weeks).

- You're feeling better and better about them, and you've grown closer to them after each date.

If all of these are true for you, then you're ready to move forward into a committed relationship! You may feel like this has been a lot of work and a big investment, and you probably feel like you've never talked through that much with someone you're dating—all *before* you're even in an official relationship.

But, as we discussed in Date Nine, you have to do this work before making a commitment to ensure you're not allowing your emotions to cloud your judgment. You're bringing your head along for the journey since your heart is looking for love.

Ideally, this ten-date journey has lasted anywhere from two to three months, averaging one date a week early on and then two dates per week around Date Five. Many people ask me if the length of time really matters. The truth is, it's not so much the length of time that matters. It's what happens *in that time period* that truly counts. You can go on ten surface-level dates with someone and not be anywhere near ready to shift into a relationship. Or you can go on three deep and intentional dates with someone but not know whether they will show up the same way on Date Ten as they did on Date Three.

The goal is a relationship that you both intentionally choose, not one that you slide into by default. Too often people commit to a relationship—or even marry someone—simply because it seems like the logical next step. I say this with all the love and empathy in the world: It is never logical to enter a committed relationship with someone who doesn't *choose* to commit to you or who isn't excited to be with you.

I am often asked, "I've been dating someone for six months. Should we be in an official relationship at this point?" If you're truly going about dating in an intentional way and you and your date have the same vision for the future, then once you pass the three-month mark, you're already likely acting like you're in a committed relationship; you're just bypassing the labels. Which begs the question, Do labels matter? To that I respond with an emphatic *yes*!

A common problem with modern dating is that we often treat someone as if they're our partner from Date One. We tell them what we prefer ("I like getting texts every morning!"), and we hope they can meet our needs, even though they haven't proven themselves a trustworthy person to communicate those needs to yet. This is often the dynamic that leads to what modern dating culture has coined a "situationship"— not quite a relationship, not quite a friendship, but there *is* a "situation" happening between the two of you.

When this happens, it feels like you're already in a relationship long before you have an obvious transition and intentional conversation. You keep going along, playing house, but ultimately, you may realize that the person you're with isn't as interested in a committed relationship as you hoped they were.

Someone's initiative to intentionally transition into a committed relationship is proof that their *desire* for a long-term relationship matches their behavior and that they have the *ability* to enter the kind of commitment they say they crave.

A lot of people think they want a relationship. They like the idea of it. But when the rubber meets the road, for whatever reason, they can't make that shift. It may be because of their attachment style. Maybe they lean toward avoidance and they're afraid that an actual label or commitment may ruin what seems like a great connection. It may be because they want to keep their options open and they're succumbing to what we talked about in Date One: the paradox of choice. They think you're great, but what if there's someone *greater*?

Relationship expert Jillian Turecki says it best: "People spend too much time analyzing the emotionally unavailable person and not enough time walking away from them."[1]

Someone may have checked all the boxes on your list, but for whatever reason, they can't or won't transition into a commitment. At this point, the best thing to do is walk away if they're not ready and they can't tell you why. As painful as that may be, you can be thankful that you've discovered this before you've committed to a relationship with them.

Soul Work

The Art of Commitment

It's at the tender beginning of a new relationship when true fear of commitment tends to emerge. What makes someone afraid of commitment? According to research, it tends to be not one thing but rather a combination of factors that leads people to fear and to avoid commitment.

Negative experiences, such as betrayal or abandonment in

past relationships, can often influence individuals' perceptions of trust and commitment in future relationships.[2] People with insecure attachment styles (such as anxious or avoidant) often struggle with intimacy and commitment. Some individuals fear being vulnerable or emotionally exposed.[3] Others fear losing independence or autonomy. Research has found that partners often vary regarding how much independence they desire in a relationship. If they've often wanted more independence than their partner, especially in past relationships, this may indicate that their fear of commitment stems from fear that they will lose their independence.[4]

Some research suggests that those with low self-esteem tend to fear commitment. The reasons for this can vary, but it makes sense that if someone lacks confidence in themselves, they're hesitant to make a commitment because they're not sure they can be who they want to be in that relationship. And they often don't believe in themselves enough to think they can cocreate a healthy relationship, even if they think the other person is amazing.[5]

Or maybe one of you is afraid to commit because you've gone through the ten-date process by merely going through the motions or you've overlooked some red flags that showed up early on. If that's the case, I encourage you to have grace for yourself and to be thankful for the opportunity to learn through this experience by gaining clarity and perspective.

If you notice that you want to delay this conversation or you feel that the person you're dating does, one of you may have a deep-seated fear of commitment. One way to know is to go back to the conversations you've had about past relationships. Was a fear of commitment ever expressed? What about any hint of a pattern of short-term, unstable relationships, betrayal, or abandonment? You never want to have to convince someone to commit to you. Simultaneously, be aware of patterns of self-sabotage, especially if all the boxes seemed to be checked but now, suddenly, one of you doesn't "feel" ready for a relationship.

We all have the potential to self-sabotage a great relationship. Sometimes it's because of our fear of failure; other times it's because of what author Gay Hendricks refers to as our "fear of success."[6] Sometimes we're afraid of what will happen if this relationship *does* work out. We'd have to let go of all our beliefs about how there are "no good guys left" or that "relationships are for the weak" or whatever false belief was getting us through our single years.

We've become comfortable with our beliefs, no matter how negative they are. We've become accustomed to "relational failure" (*oof*—harsh, but that's what it feels like). And the challenging thing is, when it comes to dating, it all feels like failure—the whole journey—until suddenly it doesn't and it ends with success!

How do we go from identifying as a dating failure, fearing that no one will ever love us and that we're destined to end up alone, to suddenly being in a healthy relationship? It's a big shift for our nervous system, our identity, and our internal beliefs. In most other areas, we can shift our beliefs gradually. But when it comes to relationships, this shift often happens suddenly as we transition from being single to being in a relationship.

Strategy

Express, Don't Expect

The process of this transition to making your relationship official is simple. Maybe the other person has even brought up this conversation before Date Ten, which works as well! It's not an exact science; it's more about ensuring that you've crossed your t's and dotted your i's, having learned holistically about them over time.

If they ask you to be their girlfriend at this point but you haven't yet asked them about their mental health, I recommend saying something like, "I'm feeling the same, and I'd love to. But I do have a few questions about some things if you're open to answering them before we're officially in a relationship."

After you've had that conversation, you can feel confident and comfortable moving forward.

As my client Sara experienced in past relationships, she often hadn't had enough time to learn about a person in different contexts or observe their character, ensuring it was consistent over a period of time. One month isn't long enough to gather the information about and have the experiences with a person that you need before deciding to commit to them.

Additionally, many people who are emotionally unhealthy or unavailable for a relationship—or, worst-case scenario, who are emotionally manipulative—tend to rush into a commitment because they're afraid someone won't want to be with them otherwise.

When you are approaching this conversation, expressing yourself clearly is always the best way to go. You can simply make a statement like this: "I've really enjoyed getting to know you over the last several months, and I'm open to taking our relationship into a commitment."

Period. Full stop.

If you're a woman who would prefer the man to make the moves but also don't want to waste your time waiting, focus on speaking from your heart but leave the statement open-ended instead of asking if they're interested. It's less directive and more expressive and gives the other person space to be themselves, to make the decision that works best for them without feeling pressured to do otherwise.

Usually, you'll hear one of two responses at this point: "I've been thinking the same thing, and I'd love to! Will you be my girlfriend?" Or "I've loved getting to know you as well, but I don't know if I'm ready for that commitment yet."

Most likely, you won't hear what I think of as the third response, which goes a little something like this: "I'm not interested in a relationship at this point."

Granted, it's no fun at all if that's what you end up hearing. But it's important to take it in because they've communicated to you what their long-term vision is—and unfortunately, it doesn't include a committed relationship with you. It can be confusing if they've been continuing with the intentional dates and moving the relationship and connection consistently forward. At the end of the day, if you're not part of their vision for the future, you don't want to try to elbow your way in there. That road generally won't lead to a relationship full of mutual love, care, and understanding.

Okay, let's back up a minute to the second option you might hear: "I've loved getting to know you as well, but I don't know if I'm ready for that commitment yet."

If you receive this response, you may feel like you've been led on or feel embarrassed at this "rejection." Resist the urge to panic or go into blame-shifting mode. Rather than going that route, the best thing to do is to say something like, "Thanks for sharing that with me. What would you need to know about me or what would need to happen to shift into a committed relationship?"

Stay curious. Maybe they have unanswered questions. Maybe they want to go on a few more dates with you. Whatever the answer is, the key here is to notice if there is ambiguity in their response. Is there really something they need clarity on, or are they avoiding a deeper commitment and vulnerability? Is it about you, or is it a pattern in their behavior?

The main thing to focus on here on Date Ten—if they aren't ready for that commitment—is figuring out what they need from you to feel ready to move forward. If there's a tangible, actionable step you can take—like going on a few more dates or providing additional clarity about your past relationships or meeting their friends or family—then great! Move forward and check in after those needs are met.

However, if you get a general "I don't know" response, I recommend asking some questions about their past relationships. Is this something they've felt before? Do they tend to have fears about commitment? What are those fears?

Again, the key is not to take it personally or internalize this perceived rejection. It likely has nothing to do with you.

At this point, they've enjoyed your company enough to go on these ten intentional and integrative dates to learn who you are and to determine if they can see a future with you.

If someone can't make the shift, it's not you, it's them.

Finding Love the Feminine Way

Women often ask me how to stay in their "feminine energy" while also guiding the much-needed conversations about what comes next. I find that what women usually mean by this is that they want to attract someone who adheres to more traditional gender roles. These women often want a man who is going to lead and pursue them every step of the way.

On the one hand, I think this trend is positive in many ways and is a natural response to a mindset that has existed at the opposite extreme for so long. On the other hand, people often confuse being feminine with being powerless and passive. If you look at Scripture, you'll find that the women of the Bible were anything but passive.

From Ruth, to Esther, to Abigail, to Jael (this biblical Xena the Warrior Princess literally killed some dude with a tent peg while he was sleeping!), something tells me these women weren't wasting their days waiting by the phone for some dude to text them back. These women were powerful, even when living in a time and society designed to disempower them. These founders of femininity were truly committed to protecting their time and their energy and doing meaningful, transformational work that mattered.

Which is why I say, when we express what we're feeling, we're accessing what it means to be a woman. We are tapping into our center and speaking the truth from the heart, knowing that no matter what, we are worthy.

In my belief, the true picture of the feminine woman is painted in Proverbs 31. This woman was *busy*. She had a full life that she really seemed to enjoy. And she was anything but passive (or passive-aggressive). While she loved and honored her husband, she didn't seem to wait around for him or rely on him to do anything.

She made her own decisions: "She considers a field and buys it" (Proverbs 31:16). The text doesn't say, "She waited for her husband's approval before she decided which field to buy, because he was the one who knew about the fields and all she knew about were fancy purses." Right at the start of the passage we read, "Her husband has full confidence in her" (Proverbs 31:11).

Wow. Full confidence. Why? Probably because she was strong in her own identity and worth. That trust was built over time. Making decisions together. Trusting each other.

And in the early stages of their relationship, that trust was likely born of the ability to be open, honest, and vulnerable with each other. Not hiding what she was feeling because she wanted a man to make the first move. Nope. Not this power couple.

Unfortunately, in our effort to be "feminine," many of us women have lost the plot and lost our power. Being feminine is about being connected to our heart, being vulnerable, and being real. It's not about controlling another person. We desire and allow our partner to be fully themselves. It's about flowing with life and connecting to our full potential. Being in a relationship that supports us as we also support each other.

It's independence and interdependence.

It's important not to lose sight of that just because you're waiting for him to say the perfectly romantic thing first. You should have an overall feeling of mutual love and support, and you also should feel that he is interested in you and pursuing you. We often get so caught up in the story of how we met and who made the first move that we overlook the substance of the relationship we're trying to form. And don't take my word for it—the research says the same thing.

According to the dating app OkCupid, message threads started by women tend to evolve into lengthier conversations, and women who take the initiative to send the first message tend to end up with partners who are more attractive, compared to those who wait for incoming messages.[7] A survey from *The League* recently found that one out of three of the happy couples who met on their app said it was the woman who messaged first. In another study, researchers found that 72 percent of men said they preferred that women make the first move.[8]

Is our generation full of lazy men?

I'd beg to differ. I think there is potential for dating fatigue for *anyone*. The number of choices we have, combined with technology burnout, makes it challenging for men to always be expected to initiate—and always to be the one who is potentially rejected first. Research has found that many people don't truly know when someone is flirting with them, or they detect flirtatious behavior incorrectly.[9]

Should men be the ones initiating the "are we ready to be in a committed relationship" conversation? Maybe.

But by expressing that they are open to a relationship,

women make it easier for that "ask" to feel natural. We can't expect the other person to read our minds, and if we want a healthy relationship down the road, initiating clear, direct, and honest communication is the way to go.

As Brené Brown shares in her research on vulnerability and trust, "Trust is a product of vulnerability that grows over time and requires work, attention, and full engagement. Trust isn't a grand gesture—it's a growing marble collection. . . . We need to trust to be vulnerable and we need to be vulnerable to build trust."[10]

By demanding vulnerability we're not willing to give—because we're stuck in "who should go first" land—we block ourselves from creating the relationship we desire.

I'm always surprised when people say they want an authentic, trusting, and communicative relationship but they're convinced the way to get there is by playing games, playing hard to get, and not expressing how they feel.

If you've seen that "marble collection" grow over time, then the person you're dating has done their part to make you feel safe and you can feel confident vulnerably expressing how you feel.

 **Tools**

Me to We

No matter who you choose to spend the rest of your life with, the merging of two identities forms a third, separate entity.

I've found that many people don't talk about this until marriage. But in my opinion, the identity shift from "me" to "we" should start right here, when you decide you want to pursue a committed relationship with someone.

Often our "fear of success" includes a belief that there is a sort of "death" with this new "birth" of a relationship. The death that occurs is your loss of identity as a single person. As much as you complained about being single and desperately prayed to be in the position you're now in, there were things you loved—or learned to love—about being single. And now there will be things to let go of and grieve at the loss of your single identity.

This loss may be compounded by your uncertainty about whether this relationship will go the distance. This is the point where many people self-sabotage a budding relationship.

Now, to be clear, I'm not saying that just because you made it to Date Ten and want to pursue a committed relationship, there's no going back. Not at all. But many people don't realize they're afraid of letting go of their identity as a single person and truly embracing the new relationship—and this fear affects their relationship.

What if it doesn't work out? This may be the question in the back of our minds. It's a reasonable concern, but this very worry could be what makes the relationship *not* work out. (This is the same dynamic we talked about when we went from Date One to Date Two. If you assume it's not going to work out, you don't show up open, available, and ready.)

It's important not to make this assumption when you are

transitioning into an official relationship on Date Ten. How do you keep from sabotaging your new relationship?

First, identify and describe your "single identity." What are the positives—the things you liked about being single? Close your eyes, take a few deep breaths, and notice where in your body you feel expanded and open when you think about singleness. Maybe images come up of embarking on solo travel adventures, having fun with friends, sleeping in, and not needing to worry about anyone else's schedule or meet anyone else's needs.

Next, consider any fear of success you've had about relationships. Ask yourself, "What do I fear would happen if I entered this committed relationship and it was successful? What thing that I love about being single am I afraid to lose? Where did this belief originate?"

Maybe your mom gave up her career when she got married or felt hidden resentment toward her children because she sacrificed her own identity and didn't enjoy her life. In reality, however, there may have been reasons for her unhappiness that you were unaware of. And that was a different era when women often felt pressured to choose between a career and a family. You have to realize that this doesn't happen in every relationship. You can choose a different path.

Maybe you're afraid your work performance will suffer because you believe you can't have career success *and* a happy and healthy relationship.

Maybe you're afraid you'll lose your freedom.

Maybe you're afraid that someone will have control over your life, and you like being in control.

Whatever your fear is, now is the time to address it.

Finally, review the facts about the person you're dating to help offset your fears. If you're afraid of having to give up your career, recall conversations you've had about this, and remind yourself of how he's shown interest in your goals, engaged in conversations about your career, and offered you support. Typically, our fears aren't based on facts about the situation but rather are an emotional or protective response stemming from a prior experience that has shaped our belief system.

When You Know, You Know

If you've gone through the steps laid out in this chapter, had *the* conversation, and now find yourself in an official relationship with a significant other, congratulations!

I couldn't be happier for you! Not just because you've found success through what you've learned in this book, but more so because you can feel confident that you've done the soul work, implemented the right strategies, used the best tools, asked the needed questions, and learned to rely on more than a feeling to determine if someone is the right person for you.

This is far more than most people do before they enter a marriage, let alone a relationship! Because of your hard work, you've likely set yourself up for not just any relationship but a happy and healthy relationship. Date Ten isn't the end of the process, though. In many ways, it's just the beginning. Now the real work begins.

When I led Sara through the ten-date journey in her growing relationship with Ben, she was fearful she might overlook some warning signs in the process. She was wary of committing yet again, only to have the rug pulled out from under her. She was scared of getting involved with yet another guy, only to have him not be who he said he was—and who she thought he was.

What she found, though, was that the relationship she entered with Ben was different from any other relationship she had experienced before. Going through the ten-date process helped her develop the safety she'd been longing for with a guy, so much so that what used to feel like a risk ended up feeling like rest.

Like letting out a sigh of relief instead of holding her breath through the whole relationship.

Like reminding the little girl inside her that she was worthy of being chosen.

While every relationship has risks, that's not a reason for us to jump in feetfirst with a blindfold covering our eyes. We want to take the *right* risks. We want to learn what we can about a person, eyes wide open. We want to have grace for someone else's flaws and imperfections without playing Russian roulette with the most important decision of our lives.

When it comes to commitment, our fears tend to step forward, our hesitations about letting go of parts of our identity take center stage, and our growing pains in transitioning from "me" to "we" drive the bus.

But when we *do* create that bond—that connection characterized by trust and safety and the vulnerability that develops over time—we find that within the security of commitment, we have permission to blossom into who we truly are. The person we become after Date Ten is someone worth noting as we ask ourselves, "Who am I when I am well loved? Who am I when my needs for connection, love, and trust are met?"

You don't only get to know the person across from you with whom you've traveled this ten-date journey; you also get to meet a new version of yourself—a connected and loved version of you who is finally in a committed and healthy relationship.

You may be surprised by how she relaxes into love, this former Miss Independent, "I don't need no man" boss babe.

You may be surprised by how she softens into love, this former black coffee–drinking jaded realist.

You may be surprised by how she warms up to love and basks in its glow instead of hiding from its light because she feels unworthy and lets shame keep her in the shadows.

Be sure to ask yourself, "Do I like this version of myself in love?" and "Can I embrace all of myself with the same grace, love, and joy I desire from my partner?"

On Date Ten, you find yourself at the beginning of transitioning from "me" to "we."

From an individual to a unit.

From looking, as Philippians 2:4 says, "not only to your own interests, but also to the interests of others" (MEV).

From looking at each other and saying, "Can I see myself with this person?" to looking at the future with this person by your side.

The Road to Love Less Traveled

If you've walked this journey, with this road map, you have truly taken what poet Robert Frost referred to as the road less traveled. In case you need a quick American Lit refresher, Robert Frost described two different roads in perhaps his best-known poem. At the time, he didn't know if he'd taken the right road, so to speak. But we find him at the crossroads:

> Two roads diverged in a yellow wood,
> And sorry I could not travel both.

He looks as far as he can down the path of one road, and try as he might, he can't tell which one is better or worse. The interesting part of the poem, for me, is at the end, where he says,

> I shall be telling this with a sigh
> Somewhere ages and ages hence:
> Two roads diverged in a wood, and I—
> I took the one less traveled by,
> And that has made all the difference.[11]

Following this process is surely the "road less traveled" in the world of modern dating. But it will truly make all the difference. Because being in the right relationship and marrying the right person is the most important decision of your life.

Coaching Corner

The date: Of all the dates you've been on, this is the one that could bring the biggest change. Make it someplace special, somewhere you can talk and reflect.

Ideal amount of time: The world is your oyster!

Ideal settings: A picnic under the stars, a romantic dinner, a boat ride or dinner cruise—anywhere that allows you to have a deep conversation.

Dos: Be vulnerable and authentically yourself. Keep things lighthearted and joyful. Just because the relationship is about to become serious doesn't mean you have to be!

Don'ts: You're not here to pressure the other person to take a leap into a relationship or for you to feel pressured to do so. With honesty, honor, and hope, you're here to discover what the next chapter is for this relationship.

The DTR on Date Ten

This is the time when the conversation about moving the relationship forward will be happening. Whether you are bringing up the DTR talk or they are, express your feelings with candor and without pressure.

Questions to Ask on Date Ten
- What are you looking forward to about a potential next chapter in our relationship?

- What, if any, concerns do you have about moving forward into a committed relationship?
- Is there anything else you'd like to know about me that you haven't already asked?
- What does being in a committed relationship mean to you?

Post-Date Ten Reflections
- Was I able to give an honest expression of where my heart and head are right now?
- What have I learned from this experience?
- How would I describe my relationship with this person at this moment?
- What am I looking forward to continuing to learn about them in this next chapter of our relationship?

By reaching the end of this journey, you've committed to taking the "road less traveled" in the world of modern dating. It will truly make all the difference as you embark on a new and exciting journey from me to we.

Conclusion

As we reach the end of our journey together through *10 Dates to Your Soulmate*, I want to remind you that it's also the beginning of your journey into a healthy, life-giving relationship. We are designed for relationships, connection, and intimacy, and though there are different ways to arrive at the intended destination or finish line, the 10-Date Method will help create the relationship you desire.

My hope for you, in moving forward, is that you enjoy the journey as much as you enjoy the arrival to the love you've been searching for. If you follow all I've shared with you, the dating process is sure to feel magical instead of mundane. Dating should be anything but painful: the happy ending shouldn't justify the miserable middle. Instead, the goal should be for the dating process to look a lot like the final destination: authentic, loving, grace-filled, vulnerable, and fulfilling.

To some, ten dates may seem like a short amount of time to know if someone is "the one," and to others it may feel like a lifetime. The truth is, it's not about the time that passes; it's about what happens in the time you spend together that counts. By applying the soul work, strategies, tools, and processes you learned in this book, you'll surely be "making the most of every opportunity" (Ephesians 5:16) as you await the love coming your way.

I'm honored that you've chosen to embark on this journey toward finding enduring love with this book as your guide. I'd like to leave you with a powerful sentiment from the esteemed John Steinbeck. These words were a constant source of inspiration and hope during my dating journey, and I pray they provide the same for you. Steinbeck penned these words in a letter to his son, Tom, as he navigated his own new relationship: "If you are in love, that's a good thing—that's about the best thing that can happen to anyone. Don't let anyone make it small or light to you. . . . And don't worry about losing. If it's right, it happens—The main thing is not to hurry. Nothing good gets away."[1]

I hope these words resonate with you as they did with me. Remember, if it's meant to be, it will find a way. Indeed, nothing good gets away!

Acknowledgments

This book on helping others find love has truly been a labor of love, and many people have supported me along the way.

I first would like to thank my Lord Jesus for his continuous love. "We love because he first loved us" (1 John 4:19). It is because of his love that we can experience and truly enjoy abundant and precious love. He has guided my path that has led to my purpose and legacy of love through my work here on earth.

I would like to thank my husband, Joah, for being my constant support and inspiration. From the time we met as kids at vacation Bible school to having our own ten-dates-to-your-soulmate journey: You're the answer to all my prayers, and you've gifted me with the support and belief that have helped me build my company and do the work I do today.

For the constant joy he brings, I'd like to thank my son, Caleb, for teaching me how to have a childlike faith and love for others and the world around me. You've changed my definition of love forever. I've never known love like I do now, being your mother.

For their unwavering support and encouragement since I was a child, I'd like to thank my parents, Kev and Ayline Tcharkhoutian. Your beautiful love set the foundation for who I am and what I do today. I always knew it was a special love, but I never knew how rare it was. When people wonder if true love and happiness still exist, I always and forever can lean on the inspiration I have from your relationship. Thank you for your constant support and belief in me. The sacrifices made by you, your parents, and the generations before us have given me the opportunities I have today.

To my sister and best friend. Looking up to you from a young age, and still today as a mom, I am forever grateful that you taught me the power of love and friendship and always believed I could do anything and that I was worthy of great love, even in my disappointing dating days. I thank God every day that you're the best friend he chose for me.

To my family and friends, including my nephews James and Joshua, my niece Joelle, the Kederians, the suities, my Bible study life group, the Armenian community, and my team that helps our clients find love every day: It truly took a village to write this book, and I'm grateful to have the best village there is.

To our amazing clients who have put their trust in us to help them on the most vulnerable and important journey of their lives, the journey to find love: Thank you for trusting me. Your hope, your perseverance, your faith, and your love stories inspire me daily.

This book would not have been possible without the vision and guidance of my amazingly skillful and gifted editor, Keren Baltzer, and the team at Zondervan. You truly championed my vision and brought it to life. Working with you has been a match made in heaven.

To Rachel Jacobson and the team at Alive Literary Agency: Thank you for believing in me and supporting me in every step of the process. And to my editors, Julie Carr and Janna Walkup, thank you for helping me learn how to listen to my own voice. As a first-time author, I am grateful for your invaluable support.

A special thank-you to Dr. Neil Clark Warren and the team at eHarmony for starting my journey as a matchmaker and teaching and inspiring me to help others find true, lasting, and compatible love.

This book is in memory of my paternal grandfather, Noubar Tcharkhoutian, a prolific Armenian fiction author, and my maternal grandmother, Analee Euredjian, a cherished teacher. Their profound influences in the realms of writing and education have been my guiding light as I crafted this work, which embodies the lessons I share with my clients.

My grandfather Noubar ignited in me a deep-seated passion for writing and reading. His legacy inspired my aspirations to become an author. My grandmother Analee's dedication to teaching has shaped my approach, fueling my commitment to impart knowledge to my clients daily. This book represents their wildest dreams come true, and it is because of their legacy—commitment to family and to their craft—that I, the daughter and granddaughter of Lebanese-Armenian immigrants, have the opportunities I do today.

About the Author

Dr. Christie Kederian is an internationally renowned relationship expert, therapist, speaker, and thought leader. With an extensive career as a professional matchmaker and relationship expert for eHarmony and other dating sites, Dr. Christie has helped thousands of people create lives they love and find love they deserve.

She is a "Triple Trojan," receiving her bachelor's, master's, and doctoral degrees at the University of Southern California in psychology and marriage and family therapy. She has been a featured expert on ABC, NBC, and FOX and in *The Wall Street Journal, Los Angeles Times*, and many more.

She lives in a small town outside Los Angeles with her loving husband, sweet two-year-old son, and cocker spaniel, Lady (yes, named after the Disney movie). She loves playing the bass guitar, enjoying live music, hiking with a matcha in hand, and globe-trotting every chance she gets.

Notes

Date One: One-and-Done or Found the One?

1. Edward O. Laumann, John H. Gagnon, Robert T. Michael, and Stuart Michaels, *The Social Organization of Sexuality: Sexual Practices in the United States* (Chicago: University of Chicago, 1994), 235.
2. Barry Schwartz, *The Paradox of Choice: Why More Is Less* (New York: Harper Perennial, 2004).

Date Two: It Takes Two (Dates) to Tango

1. R. S. Nickerson, "Confirmation Bias: A Ubiquitous Phenomenon in Many Guises," *Review of General Psychology* 2, no. 2: 175–220, https://doi.org/10.1037/1089 -2680.2.2.175.
2. Evan Marc Katz, "Believe the Negatives, Ignore the Positives," *Evan Marc Katz Blog*, accessed April 25, 2024, https://www .evanmarckatz.com/blog/understanding-men/believe-the -negatives-ignore-the-positives.
3. Gili Freedman, Janell C. Fetterolf, and Jennifer S. Beer, "Engaging in Social Rejection May Be Riskier for Women," *Journal of Social Psychology* 159, no. 5 (2019): 117, https:// doi.org/10.1080/00224545.2018.1532388.

4. "Ram Dass Quotes," Ram Dass, October 19, 2021, https://www.ramdass.org/ram-dass-quotes/.

5. James B. Moran, Courtney L. Crosby, Taylor Himes, and T. Joel Wade, "Dating Around: Investigating Gender Differences in First Date Behavior Using Self-Report and Content Analyses from Netflix," *Sexuality and Culture* 27, no. 5 (May 2023): 1–23, https://doi.org/10.1007/s12119-023-10086-y.

6. E. E. Jones and T. S. Pittman, "Self-Presentation and Social Influence: Evidence for an Automatic Self-Presentation Mechanism," in J. Suls, ed., *Psychological Perspectives on the Self*, vol. 1 (Mahwah, NJ: Erlbaum, 1982), 231–62.

Date Three: Third Time's a Charm?

1. Erving Goffman, *The Presentation of Self in Everyday Life* (Garden City, NY: Doubleday, 1959).

2. A. Aron, C. C. Norman, E. N. Aron, et al., "Couples' Shared Participation in Novel and Arousing Activities and Experienced Relationship Quality," *Journal of Personality and Social Psychology* 78, no. 2 (February 2000): 273–84, https://doi.org/10.1037//0022-3514.78.2.273.

3. Justin A. Lavner, Benjamin R. Karney, and Thomas N. Bradbury, "Does Couples' Communication Predict Marital Satisfaction, or Does Marital Satisfaction Predict Communication?" *Journal of Marriage and Family* 78, no. 3 (June 1, 2016): 680–94, https://doi.org/10.1111/jomf.12301.

4. A. Aron, D. G. Dutton, and E. N. Aron, "Some Evidence for Heightened Sexual Attraction under Conditions of High Anxiety," *Journal of Personality and Social Psychology* 30, no. 4 (1974): 510–17, https://doi.org/10.1037/h0037031.

Date Four: Four Better or Worse

1. Helen Fisher, Arthur Aron, and Lucy L. Brown, "Romantic Love: An fMRI Study of a Neural Mechanism for Mate Choice," *Journal of Comparative Neurology* 493, no. 1 (December 5, 2005): 58–62, https://doi.org/10.1002/cne.20772.

2. Claus Wedekind, Thomas Seebeck, Florence Bettens, and Alexander J. Paepke, "MHC-Dependent Mate Preferences in Humans," *Proceedings: Biological Sciences* 260, no. 1359 (June 22, 1995): 245–49, https://doi.org/10.1098/rspb.1995.0087.

3. Neil Clark Warren, *The Triumphant Marriage: How to Achieve a Love That Lasts Forever* (New York: HarperCollins, 1998).

4. "The eHarmony Compatibility Score: Make Your Matches Count," eHarmony, accessed July 25, 2024, https://www.eharmony.com/tour/what-is-compatibility-system/.

5. C. S. Lewis, *The Four Loves* (New York: Harcourt Brace Jovanovich, 1960), 85.

6. "What Is Compatibility in a Relationship and How to Nurture It," eHarmony, accessed July 25, 2024, https://www.eharmony.com/dating-advice/dating/compatibility-relationship/.

7. "What Is Compatibility in a Relationship and How to Nurture It," eHarmony.

8. Zero Mostel, vocalist, "Tradition," composed by Jerry Brock, lyrics by Sheldon Harnick, on the album *Fiddler on the Roof: The Original Broadway Cast Recording*, Columbia Records, 1964.

9. John M. Gottman and Nan Silver, *The Seven Principles for Making Marriage Work* (New York: Crown Publishers, 1999), chapter 7.

Date Five: Familiar Isn't Forever

1. John Bowlby, *Attachment and Loss*, vol. 1, *Attachment* (New York: Basic Books, 1969); Mary D. Salter Ainsworth, *Infancy in Uganda: Infant Care and the Growth of Love* (Baltimore: Johns Hopkins University Press, 1967).

2. C. S. Lewis, *The Four Loves* (New York: Harcourt, 1991), 121.

Date Six: Red Flag or Carnival?

1. *Vocabulary.com Dictionary*, s.v. "red flag," accessed September 22, 2024, https://www.vocabulary.com/dictionary/red flag.

2. Corinne Reczek, Hui Liu, and Debra Umberson, "Just the Two of Us? How Parents Influence Adult Children's Marital Quality," *Journal of Marriage and Family* 72, no. 5 (October 2010): 1205–19, https://doi.org/10.1111/j.1741-3737.2010 .00759.x.

3. Cassidy M. Fry, Eva H. Telzer, and Christy R. Rogers, "Siblings as Buffers: Social Problems and Internalizing and Externalizing Behaviors across Early Adolescence," *Journal of Family Psychology* 35, no. 7 (October 2021): 939–49, https:// doi.org/10.1037/fam0000876.

4. Melanie Brown, Emma Bunton, Melanie Chisholm, Geri Halliwell, and Victoria Beckham, "Wannabe," on *Spice* (London: Virgin Records, 1996).

Date Seven: Setting the Stage for Commitment

1. Ken Kwapis, dir., "Halloween," *The Office*, season 2, episode 5 (Los Angeles: NBCUniversal Television, 2005).

2. Robert B. Cialdini and Noah J. Goldstein, "Social Influence: Compliance and Conformity," *Annual Review of Psychology*,

55 (2004): 591–621, https://doi.org/10.1146/annurev.psych .55.090902.142015.

3. Stephen M. Drigotas, "The Michelangelo Phenomenon and Personal Well-Being," *Journal of Personality* 70, no. 1 (February 1, 2002): 59–77, https://doi.org/10.1111/1467 -6494.00178.

4. "Marriage and Divorce," National Center for Health Statistics, last reviewed March 13, 2024, https://www.cdc .gov/nchs/fastats/marriage-divorce.htm.

5. *Annual Study on Mental Illness Prevalence*, NSS Behavioral Health, 2023.

6. *Annual Study on Mental Illness Prevalence*, NSS Behavioral Health, 2023.

7. Amanda Magee, "When You Marry 'The One,' You Also Marry the Family," Scary Mommy, December 18, 2015, https://www.scarymommy.com/when-you-marry-the-one -you-also-marry-the-family.

8. K. L. Fiori, A. J. Rauer, K. S. Birditt, et al., "You Aren't as Close to My Family as You Think: Discordant Perceptions about In-laws and Risk of Divorce," *Research in Human Development* 17, no. 4+ (2021): 258–73, https://doi.org/10.10 80/15427609.2021.1874792.

9. Joel Zwick, dir., *My Big Fat Greek Wedding* (Los Angeles: Gold Circle Films, 2002).

Date Eight: The House That Built Him

1. Maureen Stearns, *Conscious Courage: Turning Everyday Challenges Into Opportunities* (Seminole, FL: Enrichment Books, 2004), 15.

2. *Bruce Almighty*, directed by Tom Shadyac (2003; Universal Pictures Home Entertainment, 2003), DVD.
3. Salvador Minuchin, *The Disorganized and Disadvantaged Family: Structure and Process* (New York: Basic Books, 1967),
4. Gary Chapman, *The Five Love Languages: How to Express Heartfelt Commitment to Your Mate* (Chicago: Northfield Publishing, 1992).

Date Nine: No Bad Parts

1. Esther Perel, "Secret Formula for Desire in Long Term Relationships," interview with Lewis Howes, *The School of Greatness Podcast*, October 21, 2020, https://lewishowes .com/podcast/esther-perels-secret-formula-for-desire-in-long -term-relationships-never-cheat-again/.

Date Ten: Ten out of Ten

1. Jillian Turecki, Instagram post, August 2, 2022, https://www .instagram.com/reel/CgxnCvlgvfL/?utm_source=ig_web _copy_link.
2. L. Campbell, J. A. Simpson, J. Boldry, and D. A. Kashy, "Perceptions of Conflict and Support in Romantic Relationships: The Role of Attachment Anxiety." *Journal of Personality and Social Psychology* 88, no. 3 (2005): 510–31, https://doi.org/10.1037/0022-3514.88.3.510.
3. R. A. Emmons and L. A. King, "Conflict and Control: Goals, Feelings, and Strategies." *Journal of Personality and Social Psychology* 56, no. 4 (1989): 586–595.
4. C. Raymond Knee, Cynthia Lonsbary, Amy Canevello, and Heather Patrick, "Self-Determination and Conflict in Romantic Relationships," *Journal of Personality and Social*

Psychology 89, no. 6 (December 2005): 997–1009, https:// doi.org/10.1037/0022-3514.89.6.997.

5. Morris Rosenberg, *Society and the Adolescent Self-Image* (Princeton, NJ: Princeton University Press, 1965), 151–52.

6. Gay Hendricks, *The Big Leap: Conquer Your Hidden Fear and Take Life to the Next Level* (New York: Harper One, 2009).

7. OkCupid, "A Woman's Advantage," *Medium*, March 5, 2015, https://theblog.okcupid.com/a-womans-advantage-82d5074 dde2d.

8. Shari L. Dworkin and Lucia O'Sullivan, "Actual versus Desired Initiation Patterns among a Sample of College Men: Tapping Disjunctures within Traditional Male Sexual Scripts," *The Journal of Sex Research* 42, no. 2 (May 2005): 150–58, https://doi.org/10.1080/00224490509552268.

9. Jeffrey A. Hall, Chong Xing, and Seth Brooks, "Accurately Detecting Flirting: Error Management Theory, the Traditional Sexual Script, and Flirting Base Rate," *Communication Research* 42, no. 7 (May 2014): 939, https://doi.org/10.1177 /0093650214534972.

10. Brené Brown, *Daring Greatly: How the Courage to Be Vulnerable Transforms the Way We Live, Love, Parent, and Lead* (New York: Gotham Books, 2012), 32.

11. Robert Frost, "The Road Not Taken," in *Mountain Interval* (New York: Henry Holt and Company, 1916), 9.

Conclusion

1. John Steinbeck, *Steinbeck: A Life in Letters*, ed. E. R. Steinbeck and Robert Wallsten (New York: Penguin, 1989), 600.

From the Publisher

GREAT BOOKS

ARE EVEN BETTER WHEN THEY'RE SHARED!

Help other readers find this one:

- Post a review at your favorite online bookseller

- Post a picture on a social media account and share why you enjoyed it

- Send a note to a friend who would also love it—or better yet, give them a copy

Thanks for reading!